READING STREET
Sleuth
COMMON CORE

PEARSON

Glenview, Illinois
Boston, Massachusetts
Chandler, Arizona
Upper Saddle River, New Jersey

Acknowledgments appear on page 78, which constitutes an extension of this copyright page.

ISBN-13: 978-0-328-73059-9
ISBN-10:   0-328-73059-9
1 2 3 4 5 6 7 8 9 10 V011 16 15 14 13 12

Contents

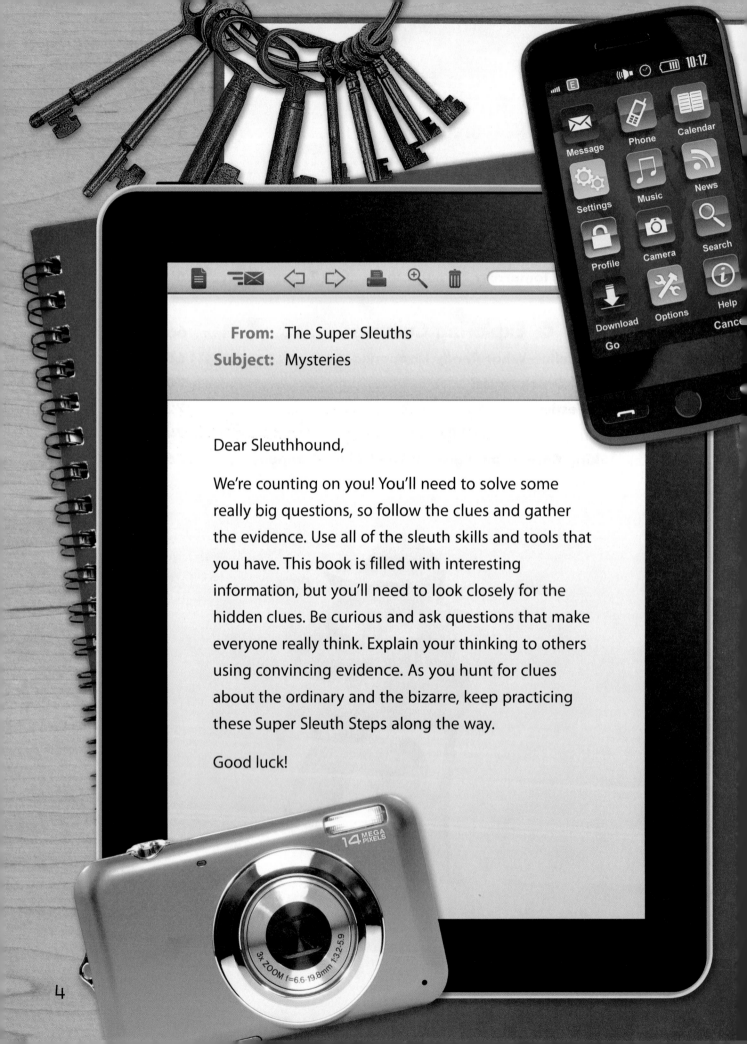

From: The Super Sleuths

Subject: Mysteries

Dear Sleuthhound,

We're counting on you! You'll need to solve some really big questions, so follow the clues and gather the evidence. Use all of the sleuth skills and tools that you have. This book is filled with interesting information, but you'll need to look closely for the hidden clues. Be curious and ask questions that make everyone really think. Explain your thinking to others using convincing evidence. As you hunt for clues about the ordinary and the bizarre, keep practicing these Super Sleuth Steps along the way.

Good luck!

SUPER SLEUTH STEPS

Gather Evidence

- Look back through the text and images. What might others have missed?

- Take good notes, create charts, or make a drawing to help you remember. All good sleuths record what they discover.

- Organize the evidence. Put the pieces together in a sequence or in categories. Look for events that cause other events.

Ask Questions

- A great question goes beyond the obvious. It makes everyone think more deeply.

- Ask about something that interests you. Super Sleuths are known for being curious.

Make Your Case

- Look at all the evidence and clues. What conclusion can you make? Be prepared to explain your thinking.

- A convincing argument includes a clearly stated position or conclusion and is supported by solid evidence. Be convincing!

Prove It!

- Think about what information is most important. Clearly show what you've learned. Prepare to be amazing!

- You might work alone or as part of a team. Everyone has something important to contribute.

Unit 1
Loyalty and Respect

Hi, Sleuthhounds! In this unit, you will be looking for clues about the meaning of loyalty and respect. Here are some sleuth tips to help you. Happy hunting!

Sleuth Tips

Gather Evidence

Why do sleuths reread?

- Sleuths know that something can be missed the first time.
- Sleuths look for details when they reread. They keep looking for clues!

Ask Questions

What makes a great question?

- Great questions are clear and focused on the topic. Sleuths ask great questions to help them learn something.
- Sleuths ask questions that will make everyone think more deeply.

Make Your Case

How do sleuths make a clear case?

- Sleuths state what they believe about a case. They state what they believe at the beginning and again at the end.
- Sleuths give reasons that are based on what they have learned. They lay out the evidence step-by-step.

Prove It!

What do sleuths do when they work with other sleuths?

- Sleuths share the evidence they have gathered.
- Sleuths share the work and the fun. They make certain everyone participates.

Welcome to BEAR COUNTRY

As long as Caroline could remember, her mom and dad had loved the outdoors. This year the whole family was going on a week-long vacation in the Adirondack Mountains. They rented a cabin deep in the woods and made plans to hike the Adirondacks, swim in the lake, and catch fish for dinner.

Nearing the cabin, Caroline pointed out a weathered sign along the road that read, "Welcome to Bear Country." She asked her father what this meant. He explained that the mountains were home not just to vacationers but also to black bears. Her father stressed that these creatures are just about as afraid of people as people are of them. "However," he told his daughter in a serious voice, "mother black bears can be fierce and will protect their cubs at all costs. If you ever find yourself between a black bear and her cubs, slowly and quietly back away without making eye contact with the bear." Caroline's heart raced with excitement as she thought about actually seeing a bear, but she was also a little wary of getting too close to one. This was going to turn out to be an exciting vacation; she felt certain.

Caroline was not to be disappointed. On their second hike, she noticed a tiny bear— tiny by bear standards at least—about twenty feet away, just to the right of the narrow

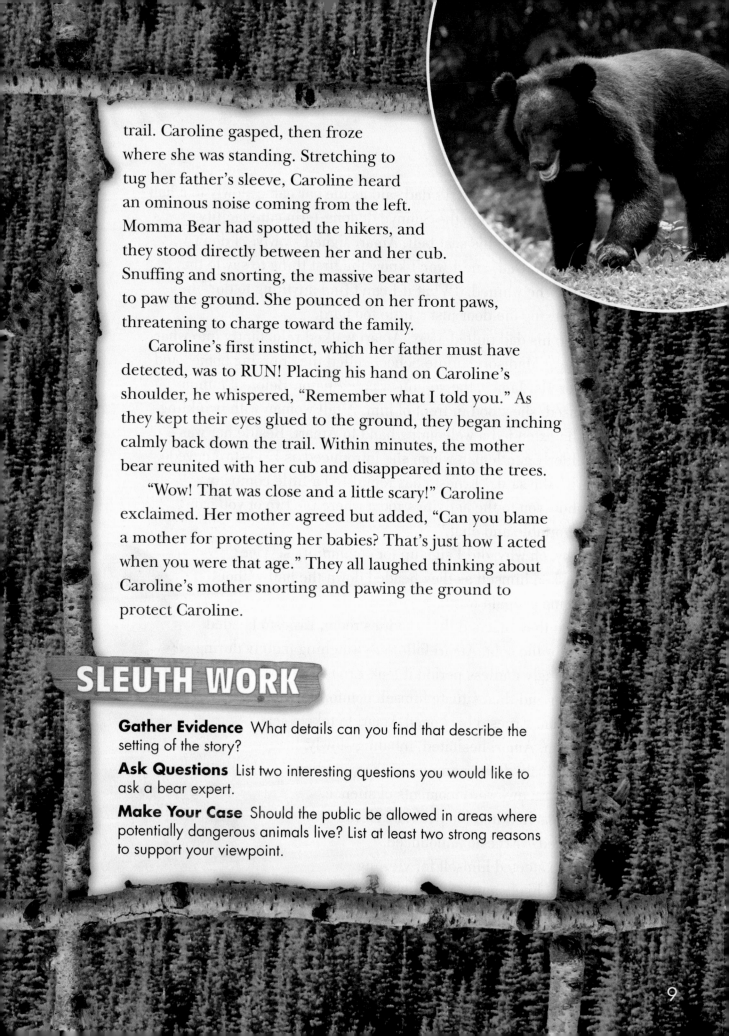

trail. Caroline gasped, then froze where she was standing. Stretching to tug her father's sleeve, Caroline heard an ominous noise coming from the left. Momma Bear had spotted the hikers, and they stood directly between her and her cub. Snuffing and snorting, the massive bear started to paw the ground. She pounced on her front paws, threatening to charge toward the family.

Caroline's first instinct, which her father must have detected, was to RUN! Placing his hand on Caroline's shoulder, he whispered, "Remember what I told you." As they kept their eyes glued to the ground, they began inching calmly back down the trail. Within minutes, the mother bear reunited with her cub and disappeared into the trees.

"Wow! That was close and a little scary!" Caroline exclaimed. Her mother agreed but added, "Can you blame a mother for protecting her babies? That's just how I acted when you were that age." They all laughed thinking about Caroline's mother snorting and pawing the ground to protect Caroline.

SLEUTH WORK

Gather Evidence What details can you find that describe the setting of the story?

Ask Questions List two interesting questions you would like to ask a bear expert.

Make Your Case Should the public be allowed in areas where potentially dangerous animals live? List at least two strong reasons to support your viewpoint.

Getting Comfortable

"Here we are," Amari's dad said as the car came slowly to a halt at the main entrance to the Sunnydale long-term care facility.

Fidgeting with his seat belt, Amari sighed slowly. "I don't want to go in, Dad, and I won't know the first thing to say to the residents," he whined. "What if I can't find anything to do?" he added, closing the door just a little too hard.

When his dad pulled away, Amari walked reluctantly into what everyone at Madison Middle School called the "nursing home" and asked for Ms. James, the volunteer coordinator. Before a minute had passed, she stood in front of him. A tall woman with twinkling eyes, she extended a welcoming hand to Amari. Beside her was a slim, elderly gentleman whom she introduced as Ernesto Acevedo. "Amari," she said, "Ernesto has requested a little company. He'll show you to the activities room where the two of you can get comfortable and chat."

"Why, oh why, did I sign up for community service?" Amari asked himself as they headed down the hall without exchanging a single word.

When they reached the activities room, Ernesto headed straight for the sofa. Amari followed, watching mutely during the seemingly endless period it took Ernesto to position his walker and then situate himself comfortably on the cushion. Ernesto beckoned Amari to take a seat beside him. Amari hesitated, inhaling slowly, his eyes nervously darting around his surroundings. After several awkward moments of silence, Ernesto reached into his pocket. "Here's what I need," Ernesto announced.

Amari steeled himself for viewing pictures of his beautiful grandchildren or lost wife (and what could he possibly say to that?), so he was surprised when

Ernesto pulled out a shiny black smartphone. "You see," Ernesto continued as he opened up an app, "I'm just not any good with this slingshot game, and I still don't understand the difference between black, white, green, and red."

Amari glanced at the smartphone and then nodded his head in excitement. He knew the game that Ernesto wanted help with. "Don't worry, Mr. Acevedo," Amari explained as he eagerly reached over to tap the screen. "I can definitely take you up to level six in no time flat!"

When Amari's dad picked him up an hour later, Amari grinned as he slid into the front seat. "Next week can I stay here a little longer?" he asked.

Sleuth Work

Gather Evidence What clues tell you that Amari's mood is different at the end of the story from what it was at the beginning? How would you explain his change in mood?

Ask Questions Where would you look to learn about community service opportunities for students in your community? List three questions to guide your research.

Make Your Case Should schools require students to do community service as part of their graduation requirements? Support your position with at least two convincing reasons.

CUBAN ADVENTURE

"I can't believe it—we're going to Cuba!" Mauricio announced to his younger brother Leon.

"Do you think Cuba is anything like New York City?" Leon asked.

"I guess we'll find out," Mauricio responded.

Although the flight to Havana lasted several hours, maneuvering through customs seemed to take even longer. Fortunately, Dad had already gotten a license to travel to Cuba. On the way to Grandmother's apartment in Old Havana, the boys stared out the taxi window. The vegetation looked strange, and the cobblestone streets lined with old buildings did not resemble the familiar New York neighborhoods. Dad explained that Old Havana was a historic area where people were renovating old buildings. That was why some places looked well-preserved but others needed work to fix a rickety structure or peeling paint.

Grandmother's bright yellow building had a bakery shop on the first floor and apartments above it. When Grandmother greeted them in front of the bakery, everyone hugged her. As they climbed upstairs to settle in, she said, "Let's relax tonight, and then I will show you boys my city."

The next morning Grandmother had her friend Mel drive them around Havana in his taxi. He pointed out sprawling museums, bustling plazas, and historic cathedrals. As they wound around the narrow streets, Mel told stories about Cuba's history. The boys were especially curious about the

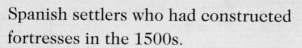

Spanish settlers who had constructed fortresses in the 1500s.

Later Mel dropped them off at the marble Fountain of Lions, where the boys played with local children and danced to the beat of bongo drums. "Follow me," Grandmother ordered as she led the way through a maze of open markets and tiny shops to a small street café, where spicy smells filled the air.

"How do you know about this place?" Mauricio asked after sampling a plate of steaming tamales.

Grandmother smiled. She answered, "I used to live in this neighborhood when I was your age." When she added, "Do you want to hear some stories about life back then?" the boys nodded eagerly, and Grandmother began reminiscing.

On the last day, Leon and Mauricio regretted having to leave because every day had been a great adventure. They had loved visiting Cuba and learning about its history and culture, but more importantly, they had made new memories with their grandmother.

SLEUTH WORK

Ask Questions What are two questions the boys might want to ask their grandmother about her experiences growing up in Cuba?

Gather Evidence List at least three places Leon and Mauricio saw and three things they did while they were in Cuba.

Make Your Case Which is a better way to learn about life in a foreign city in just one hour: taking a guided tour of the city's famous sites, or exploring on your own and eating at a local restaurant? List three convincing reasons and at least one detail from the text to support your answer.

Looking Out for Polar Bears

Want to adopt a polar bear? Now you can! Of course, the bear won't really live with you because polar bears spend most of their lives on the frozen Arctic sea ice. They are the largest land mammal that relies on the sea for food. Because polar bears are important predators in the Arctic's marine food chain, their health reflects the health of the whole ecosystem. Unfortunately, changes in the environment now threaten these magnificent animals. For example, polar bear populations in northern Canada have dropped by 20 percent since the 1990s.

Changes in the environment include rising temperatures, which have caused a serious decline in the amount of sea ice. Sea ice forms on the sea's surface when salt water freezes. Polar bears depend on sea ice to breed and rest; they also use it as a base for hunting. Seals are the bears' favorite prey, and they must come to the surface for air on a regular basis. Bears wait at openings in the ice where the seals come to the surface. Because melting sea ice has left large patches of open water, seals can surface anywhere. That makes it harder for the bears to find their main source of food.

In the past, bears searching for food could travel long distances by walking across the sea ice. Occasionally, they might swim a short distance from one solid surface to another. Now they must swim much farther or spend the summers with little food, living off their stored fat. This is especially true for females with cubs that are not strong enough for long swims and still rely on their mothers for food. For this reason, many polar bears now suffer from malnutrition or starvation.

Concerned scientists and volunteers from groups like the World Wildlife Fund (WWF) and Polar Bear International are working diligently to help polar bears. They learn more about polar bear habits by tracking individual animals, and they enlist the aid of natives who have long interacted with and respected these animals. The WWF works to protect critical habitats by stopping threats from industrial activity, such as oil and gas drilling. The organization also raises money by asking people to donate money to "adopt" an animal and pay for research.

Conservation organizations need all the help they can get. Check out ways you can help protect polar bears without even leaving your home!

Sleuth Work

Gather Evidence What clues in the text can you find that tell why the author wrote this selection?

Ask Questions List at least three questions you have about polar bears or their Arctic environment.

Make Your Case What conclusion about polar bears' future can you draw? Refer to specific evidence in the selection to justify your conclusion.

Congratulations! You are the proud new owner of three truly exotic pets: a flying squirrel, a tamarin, and a spur-thighed tortoise from Africa. You are in all probability the only person on your block with any of these pets, let alone all three. With this honor comes great responsibility, however. Your new pets will appreciate your knowing exactly how to care for them, so please pay attention!

Your flying squirrel needs a good-sized cage containing a few toys, like pieces of rope. Flying squirrels may be small, but they are very active. It's wise to include some tree branches for the animal to jump around on and a nesting box where it can sleep. Worried about what to feed your flying squirrel? Don't worry. Flying squirrels eat practically anything, including delicacies like sunflower seeds, boiled chicken, and mealworms. Beware, though. If your squirrel gets out of its cage, it may try to eat your television wires, carpet, and baseboards as well!

Then there's your new tamarin, which is a small, inquisitive, and extremely cute monkey. You can keep your tamarin in a cage, but people often find it works best to give these critters the run of the house. As for feeding, tamarins like many different kinds of food, from oatmeal to marshmallows, and they get bored with the same meal every day. For that matter, tamarins crave variety in general. Should you want a pet that doesn't, you'd best trade in your tamarin for a guppy or possibly a rock. One warning: Tamarins have been known to bite without provocation. If yours does, get yourself checked out to ensure you don't have a serious injury.

As for your tortoise, a fully-grown African spur-thighed tortoise may be 3 feet long and weigh 100 pounds, so you'll probably want to build a fenced-off enclosure, at least 10 feet on each side. Because a tortoise requires toasty temperatures and light, you should also provide it with a heat lamp. Make sure your tortoise has plenty of delicious hay, grasses, and flowers to eat. If it is hungry, it will dig its way out of the enclosure and start munching its way across the lawn. It's probably a good idea to keep your tortoise well-fed if you and your family want to maintain a tidy front yard!

So congratulations once again, and enjoy your new pets! Treat them nicely, and no doubt they will do the same for you.

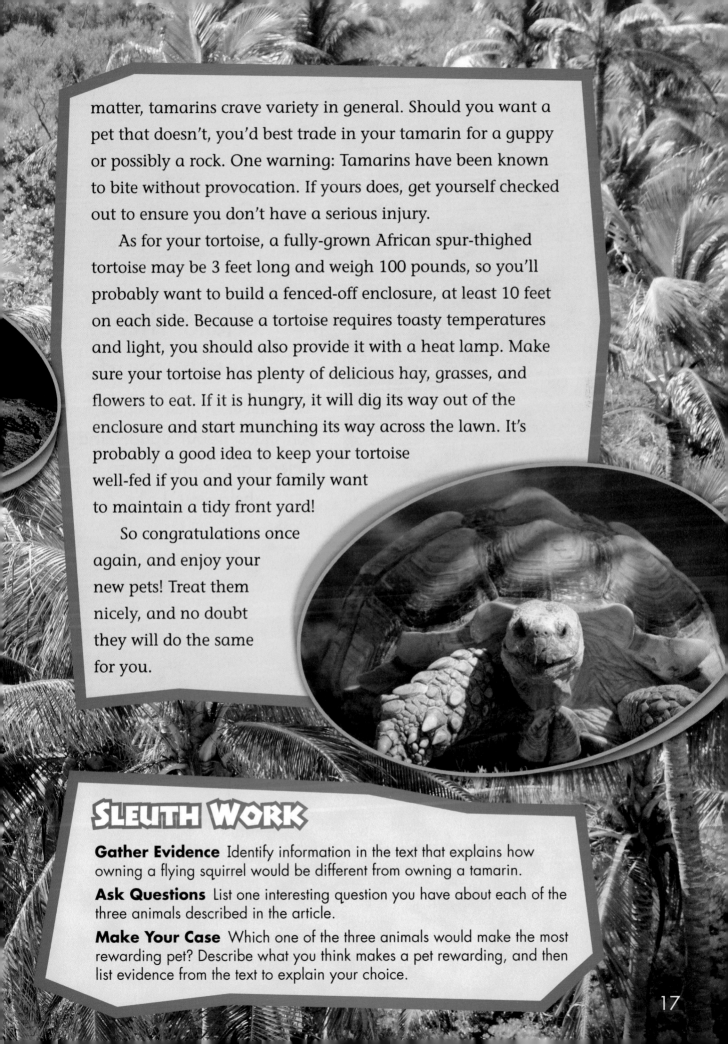

SLEUTH WORK

Gather Evidence Identify information in the text that explains how owning a flying squirrel would be different from owning a tamarin.

Ask Questions List one interesting question you have about each of the three animals described in the article.

Make Your Case Which one of the three animals would make the most rewarding pet? Describe what you think makes a pet rewarding, and then list evidence from the text to explain your choice.

Unit 2
Space and Time

Hello there, Sleuthhounds!

In this unit, you will be looking for clues about space and time. Here are some sleuth tips to help you. Let's go!

Sleuth Tips

Gather Evidence

Why do sleuths reread?

- Sleuths are always looking for clues, and they know that by rereading they might find something new and interesting.
- Sleuths focus on the details when they reread. Details, details, details!

Ask Questions

What makes a great question?

- Sleuths know that asking great questions will help to reveal new information, and so they make certain the questions are clear.
- Sleuths ask questions that may cause other sleuths to think of great ideas and more questions.

Make Your Case

How do sleuths make a clear case?

- Sleuths know that explaining their position at the start and end of a case is the best way to make a clear case.
- Sleuths present their reasons based on the facts that they have gathered and the inferences they have made.

Prove It!

What do sleuths do when they work with other sleuths?

- Sleuths share the facts and information they have gathered. They understand that other sleuths will do the same.
- Sleuths know that every sleuth should take a role in the work. They know that sharing the work can be fun!

Careers in the Space Industry

Do you like gazing at the stars on a clear night? Are you fascinated by the enormity of the universe? Do you wonder if there is life "out there"? Perhaps a career in the space industry is for you. Most of the job opportunities in space exploration or research involve science and math, but writers and artists also play a role in this exciting field.

The most common career involving space is an astronomer. Astronomers use science to study the universe. These men and women study the motions, positions, sizes, and make-up of heavenly bodies, such as stars, planets, and galaxies. Astronomers often get their doctoral degrees. Their jobs might involve teaching at a university, doing research about how something in space works, or using enormous telescopes and supercomputers to analyze how objects in space move.

Some astronomers specialize in astrophysics. That is, they study the physical and chemical measurements of heavenly bodies. The astrophysicists at the National Aeronautics and Space Administration (NASA) focus on answering three main questions: How does the universe work? How did we get here? Are we alone? These specialists use their knowledge of physics, along with advanced technology, to continue to search for answers to these questions.

If this kind of science isn't up your alley, you might be interested in another career in the space industry—engineering. Electrical engineers are responsible for designing rocket engines, propulsion devices, and satellites. They focus on the way these things will function outside Earth's atmosphere. Mechanical engineers work on any moving parts of a spacecraft, from radios to robots. They, too, have to think about the way the space environment

will affect materials. Finally, software engineers program the computers that run the spacecraft that electrical and mechanical engineers design.

If your skills are more focused in the arts, you will be happy to learn that the space industry also caters to your talents. Universities, private corporations, and government agencies all need writers to share their visions and their progress with the public. Artists might collaborate with writers to illustrate the explanations of how spacecraft work, for example.

Even if the space industry does not include the right career for you, you can still enjoy gazing at the night sky on a clear evening.

Sleuth Work

Ask Questions List two questions that you have about one of the careers described in this selection.

Gather Evidence How does the work of astronomers differ from the work of electrical engineers? Find at least three details from the text to support your answer.

Make Your Case What is the most interesting career in the space industry? Clearly state your opinion in one sentence. Then list two details from the text to support your opinion.

Journey Back in Time

Let's take a trip back in time more than 3,000 years ago to the west banks of the Nile River. Imagine working to build one of the many pyramids constructed in the rocks of Egypt's Valley of the Kings. Without iron tools, the laborers' work was difficult. It could take decades to build the complex structures; most included staircases, chambers, and narrow passageways.

The kings had the pyramids built as burial places for themselves and their families. The ancient Egyptians believed the soul lived on after death and that the bodies needed to be preserved to experience the afterlife. Furthermore, they believed that a person's possessions should be buried with the body. Through the years, thieves looted the pyramids hoping to steal gold and other treasures.

However, in 1922, Howard Carter discovered a tomb that raiders had overlooked. King Tut's burial chamber had remained almost undisturbed for thousands of years. It still contained most of the king's possessions. Besides finding the young king's mummified body, Carter discovered four rooms filled with breathtaking items. The more than 5,000 objects included Tut's gold mask and throne, jewelry, statues, and furniture. The discovery sparked widespread interest in ancient Egypt and offered important clues to the ancient Egyptians' beliefs, customs, and culture.

Now let's take another trip back in time. More than 500 years ago a city perched in the Andes (AN deez) Mountains of Peru was home to a thriving civilization. The ascent to the city was steep, almost straight up in most places. Having heard rumors of a "lost" city, historian Hiram Bingham led an expedition to the region in 1911.

On the mountain's sides, Bingham noticed stairways skillfully cut into rock and found burial caves with skeletons and well-preserved pots. His men observed the ruins of temples and houses. Machu Picchu (MAH choo PEE choo) was divided into groups of homes with one entrance and a clever locking device. Artisans had cut the locks into granite using only primitive tools.

Machu Picchu was built in the fifteenth century as an emperor's retreat. The city was an ideal refuge protected by nature. A narrow ridge on one side connected Machu Picchu to another city, but terraces had been constructed to make attack nearly impossible. Bingham's group brought back thousands of artifacts from the city. The treasures included skeletons, ceramic pottery, stoneware, bronze, and jewelry. These relics provide a fascinating glimpse into life in the Incan Empire at the height of its power.

Sleuth Work

Ask Questions What seems only partially explained in the text? Ask two factual questions you have about each ancient civilization.

Gather Evidence List evidence from the text that shows that Egyptian and Incan civilizations created objects of art and developed advanced engineering skills.

Make Your Case Do you think Howard Carter's discovery of King Tut's tomb or Hiram Bingham's exploration of Machu Picchu contributed more to our understanding of the past? Use evidence from the text to support your reasoning.

Did you know that several centuries before Christopher Columbus landed in the New World a complex civilization thrived in southern Illinois? Beginning in about A.D. 700, people settled in the rich Mississippi River floodplain near present-day St. Louis, Missouri. Over the centuries, they built a planned city, later named Cahokia (kuh HO key uh). At its peak, between the years 1050 and 1200, the city had a population between 10,000 and 20,000 people. This was larger than the city of London, England, in 1250!

Ever since archaeologists discovered ancient ruins beneath the grassy farmland, they have tried to answer questions about Cahokian culture and daily life. No written records about these people exist. Each layer of the digging site yields new clues—from pottery and buildings to burial grounds. Although researchers have learned much about the Cahokians, many mysteries remain.

One curious feature is the more than 120 earthen pyramids, known as mounds, that dot the area. The largest had a base that covered 14 acres. Named Monks Mound, it rose to the height of a 10-story building! Archaeologists estimate that this mound alone required 14 million baskets of soil. Imagine a powerful leader ordering thousands of workers to carry the baskets, one at a time! Between some mounds lie large plazas, where Cahokians may have congregated and played sports.

What each mound was used for is unclear. A large temple or palace on the highest mound may have housed a high priest. Other mounds may have contained homes, navigational landmarks, or burial grounds. Some believe that a circle of cedar posts functioned as a solar calendar, similar to Stonehenge. Researchers conclude that Cahokian astronomy was as advanced as that of other ancient civilizations.

Artifacts found hundreds of miles from Cahokia suggest a wide trade network. Some believe that Cahokia was the spiritual

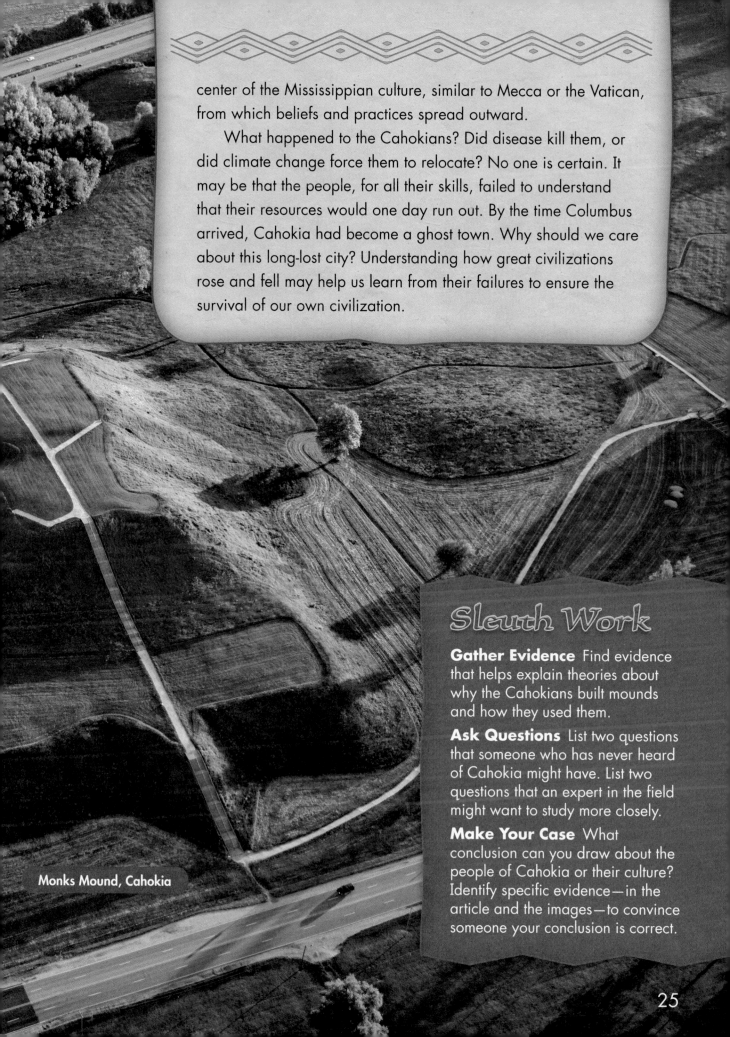

center of the Mississippian culture, similar to Mecca or the Vatican, from which beliefs and practices spread outward.

What happened to the Cahokians? Did disease kill them, or did climate change force them to relocate? No one is certain. It may be that the people, for all their skills, failed to understand that their resources would one day run out. By the time Columbus arrived, Cahokia had become a ghost town. Why should we care about this long-lost city? Understanding how great civilizations rose and fell may help us learn from their failures to ensure the survival of our own civilization.

Monks Mound, Cahokia

Sleuth Work

Gather Evidence Find evidence that helps explain theories about why the Cahokians built mounds and how they used them.

Ask Questions List two questions that someone who has never heard of Cahokia might have. List two questions that an expert in the field might want to study more closely.

Make Your Case What conclusion can you draw about the people of Cahokia or their culture? Identify specific evidence—in the article and the images—to convince someone your conclusion is correct.

25

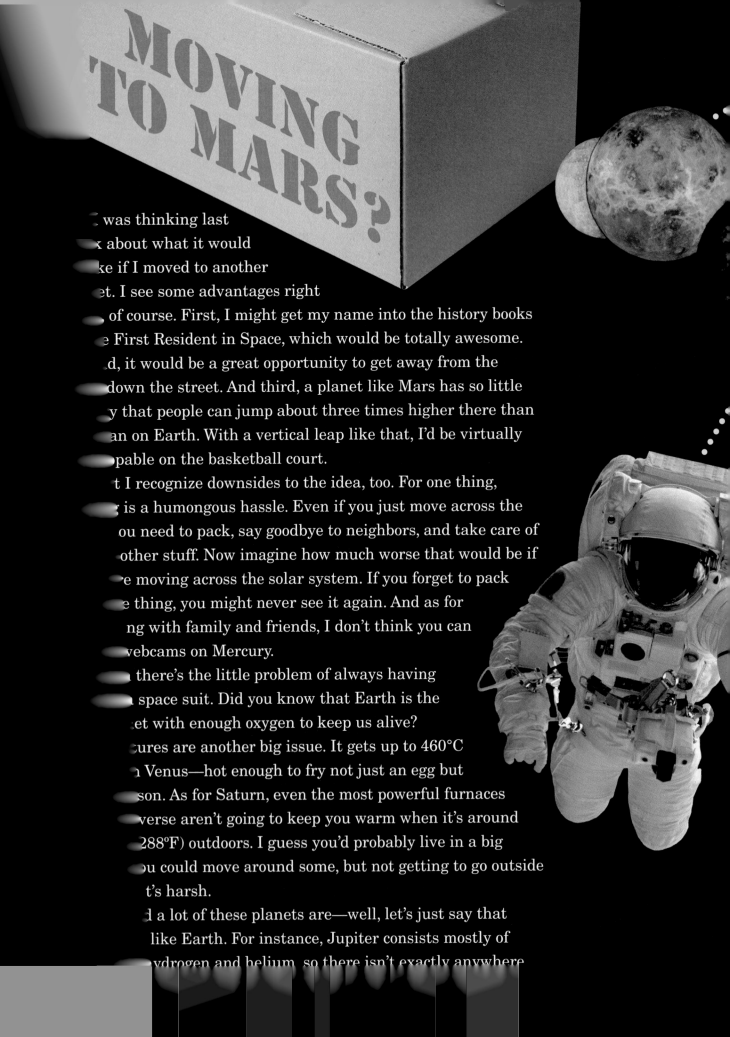

MOVING TO MARS?

was thinking last

about what it would

ke if I moved to another

et. I see some advantages right

of course. First, I might get my name into the history books

First Resident in Space, which would be totally awesome.

d, it would be a great opportunity to get away from the

down the street. And third, a planet like Mars has so little

y that people can jump about three times higher there than

an on Earth. With a vertical leap like that, I'd be virtually

pable on the basketball court.

t I recognize downsides to the idea, too. For one thing,

is a humongous hassle. Even if you just move across the

ou need to pack, say goodbye to neighbors, and take care of

other stuff. Now imagine how much worse that would be if

e moving across the solar system. If you forget to pack

e thing, you might never see it again. And as for

ng with family and friends, I don't think you can

vebcams on Mercury.

there's the little problem of always having

space suit. Did you know that Earth is the

et with enough oxygen to keep us alive?

ures are another big issue. It gets up to 460°C

Venus—hot enough to fry not just an egg but

son. As for Saturn, even the most powerful furnaces

verse aren't going to keep you warm when it's around

288°F) outdoors. I guess you'd probably live in a big

u could move around some, but not getting to go outside

t's harsh.

a lot of these planets are—well, let's just say that

like Earth. For instance, Jupiter consists mostly of

ydrogen and helium, so there isn't exactly anywhere

to stand, let alone to play basketball. Venus has almost zero water, so can you imagine the cost of trying to ship some in from Earth? And the gusts on Neptune are almost ten times stronger than the winds we get here—good for extreme kite-flying, I guess, but not for much else.

So all in all, I plan on staying here on Earth if folks begin settling the other planets. Definitely. It's the only decision that makes any sense.

SLEUTH WORK

Gather Evidence List at least three facts about the solar system the writer uses to argue against the idea of moving to a new planet.

Ask Questions Write three questions you would want to have answered about a planet before making a decision to move there.

Make Your Case How convincing is the writer's argument against settling on a new planet? To explain your answer, list specific reasons or details in the text and tell why they are or are not persuasive.

At Work on the Great Pyramid

As I pick up the clay cups, I look across the sand and spot my father chipping away at an enormous slab of limestone with his chisel. Sweat drips onto his sandals. Soon he and other masons will begin smoothing the block into the exact size the scribes require. The scribes are the bosses here at the Great Pyramid, and they will make sure the stone has the precise dimensions and perfect right angles before the laborers begin hauling it up the ramp.

My father has been working on this project every year during the flood season for fourteen years. He says the work was going on for years before he started. Father is proud of his work and prefers it to other kinds of labor for the pharaoh. After all, he is making preparations for the afterlife that each of us can have, if only we are buried correctly. And our glorious King Khufu (KOO foo) will be buried here, protected forever in this magnificent pyramid. Some say there are already two million stone blocks in the pyramid.

Although the sun is high and hot, and I have been working since it rose, I hurry back to the area where the cooks, toolmakers, and other laborers work. I hope to catch sight of my brother, but I realize that is foolish of me. With thousands of workers here, he is nowhere to be seen. Seven years ago, he started out like me, helping to get water and baskets of bread, onions, and garlic

to the workers three times a day. Now he helps pull the stone slabs from boats near the river to this great building site. The blocks weigh a few tons, and many men work together to haul them on runners.

After I return the basket of cups, a scribe directs me to see one of the cooks. As I learn from the cooks, tomorrow all the workers will enjoy a feast of fish, vegetables, and maybe even figs. I am glad that I will help prepare it. It is our ninth straight day of work, and it won't end till the sun sets, but tomorrow we will rest. If it is a good day, my father will also take home some barley seed for the new planting.

Sleuth Work

Gather Evidence What clues can you find that show how the boy and his father feel about the work they are doing at the site of the Great Pyramid?

Ask Questions List three questions you have about the Great Pyramid and how it was built. Where could you find answers to your questions?

Make Your Case Is the boy who tells the story a good source of information on the Great Pyramid? What does he know, and what doesn't he know? List specific evidence to explain and support your opinion.

Unit 3
Challenges and Obstacles

Hey, Sleuthhounds! In this unit, you will be looking for clues about challenges and obstacles. Here are some sleuth tips to help you. Get to it!

Sleuth Tips

Gather Evidence

How do sleuths get clues from images?

- Sleuths know that a picture can tell a thousand words. They gather evidence from illustrations, charts, and other visuals.
- Sleuths examine the connections between text and images. Those connections may hold clues!

Ask Questions

Why are sleuths so curious?

- Sleuths inquire and follow their instincts because they know that asking questions will lead to answers.
- Sleuths don't mind being surprised by what they learn. They are always ready to follow the next clue.

Make Your Case

Why don't all sleuths agree on the answers?

- Sleuths won't all agree on everything! They'll find different clues and put them together in different combinations.
- Sleuths realize that our differences may cause us to reach different conclusions. Diversity is important!

Prove It!

How can sleuths be creative when showing what they have learned?

- Sleuths like to "wow" their audiences. They like to present the unexpected and the unusual to show what they have discovered.
- Sleuths choose powerful and impressive words to capture the attention of the reader or listener.

Are You Thinking About a Survival Camp?

If you've ever wanted to escape the routine of your everyday life to try something new, then a weekend survival camp might be just the thing. What would convince city dwellers to venture into the wilderness for 48 hours? Well, different people have different reasons. Some are curious to try new sports, such as rafting, rock climbing, kayaking, canoeing, and fishing. Others want to learn survival skills like building a shelter and finding food and water. Still others wish to test themselves, physically and mentally, in an unpredictable and rugged environment.

Most wilderness survival programs have age and health requirements for participants. Some organizations have designed weekends especially for 12- and 13-year-olds. Some of these programs require campers to carry all their equipment in a backpack. That includes food, clothing, and tents. Each day campers hike to a different campsite that the leaders have scouted out in advance. Everyone keeps active with games, sports, and team-building exercises. Wilderness weekends generally emphasize problem-solving, physical fitness, and just plain fun. Some wilderness camps are now adding opportunities for campers to explore nature and improve the environment. Campers work under a ranger's supervision to help restore and maintain the natural habitat.

Of course, safety is always a major concern. Everyone must be prepared for the unexpected. Weather conditions can change quickly and dramatically, for example. In camps that stress survival skills, leaders and campers learn to identify water sources and edible plants in the area. Each group of hikers carries matches, a whistle or mirror for signaling, and a tin cup for heating food. Matches can be ruined by rain, so hikers practice how to create sparks by striking metal against rock or using a magnifying glass and energy from the sun. Above all, everybody learns the importance of staying calm in tough or uncertain situations.

Do weekend survival camps result in long-term benefits for young people? Do they help campers develop self-reliance, resourcefulness, or confidence—skills they can use when they return to their homes and daily routines? People certainly disagree about the answer to those questions. The truth is that not much research has been done on the long-term value and effects of wilderness camps on campers' lives. But for many people, a weekend getaway in the wilderness is an adventure of a lifetime.

Sleuth Work

Gather Evidence List key details from the text that explain the possible benefits of participating in a wilderness survival camp.

Ask Questions Ask three questions that someone who is considering going to a wilderness survival camp might want to research.

Make Your Case What conclusion about wilderness survival camps can you draw? Use text evidence to explain your reasoning and convince someone that your conclusion is correct.

Elizabeth Cady Stanton

In 1815, when Elizabeth Cady Stanton was born in Johnstown, New York, males had much more influence and many more options for employment than females in the United States. American women could not become government leaders, preachers, or professors. Girls with an interest in public speaking or politics were steered in other directions, and the law even barred women from voting. Like other girls of her time, Elizabeth was expected to become a wife and mother when she grew up—and not much else.

It's not surprising that Elizabeth Cady Stanton eventually became a wife and mother. Though she loved her family, Stanton was passionate about politics as well. One of her causes was the effort to abolish slavery in the United States. Before her marriage in 1840, she had made supporting this movement a priority. Following her marriage, moreover, she and her husband attended an antislavery conference in England.

Stanton's main concern, though, was fair treatment for women. In the mid-1800s, the laws recognized few rights of American women. Besides being barred from voting, women could not serve on juries, were denied an equal education, and could not divorce their husbands. In 1848, Stanton helped organize the Women's Rights Convention in Seneca Falls, New York. She wrote a declaration of women's rights, which was passed by the convention's delegates; this document demanded that the same rights be recognized for women as for men.

By the 1860s, Stanton was speaking and writing frequently about women's rights. Many Americans—men and women alike—disagreed with her positions. Some mocked her, while others simply ignored her. Standing strong in her beliefs, Stanton continued to travel extensively, making speeches and trying to change people's minds.

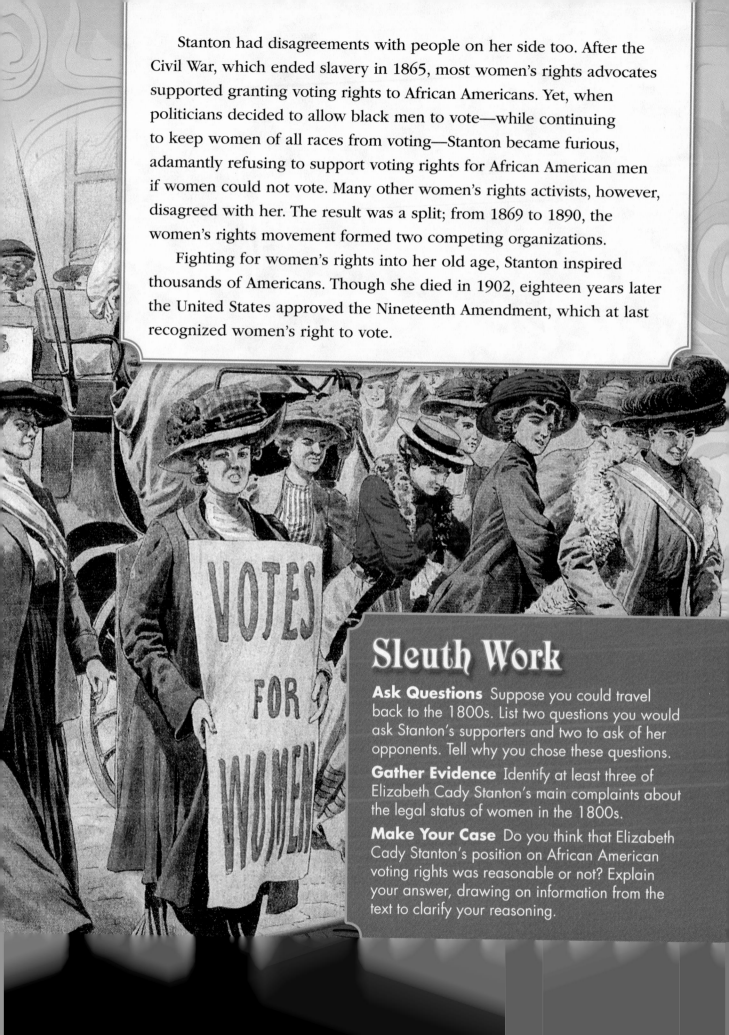

Stanton had disagreements with people on her side too. After the Civil War, which ended slavery in 1865, most women's rights advocates supported granting voting rights to African Americans. Yet, when politicians decided to allow black men to vote—while continuing to keep women of all races from voting—Stanton became furious, adamantly refusing to support voting rights for African American men if women could not vote. Many other women's rights activists, however, disagreed with her. The result was a split; from 1869 to 1890, the women's rights movement formed two competing organizations.

Fighting for women's rights into her old age, Stanton inspired thousands of Americans. Though she died in 1902, eighteen years later the United States approved the Nineteenth Amendment, which at last recognized women's right to vote.

Sleuth Work

Ask Questions Suppose you could travel back to the 1800s. List two questions you would ask Stanton's supporters and two to ask of her opponents. Tell why you chose these questions.

Gather Evidence Identify at least three of Elizabeth Cady Stanton's main complaints about the legal status of women in the 1800s.

Make Your Case Do you think that Elizabeth Cady Stanton's position on African American voting rights was reasonable or not? Explain your answer, drawing on information from the text to clarify your reasoning.

WILDERNESS MEDIC

In her teens, Sasha decided that a desk job wasn't for her. But what was? Sitting in health class one day, she became curious when Manolo, a paramedic, described his experiences being the first to respond when people are injured. He shared stories of car crashes, fires, tornadoes, and other emergencies.

When someone asked, "With all the risks, why do you do it?" Manolo paused for a minute. "First, nothing is better than seeing that you made a difference, having people express their gratitude that you were there for them during a tough time. Second, someone needs to do this work. I have a great job, and I love it, so why not me?"

Intrigued, Sasha began researching the requirements to become a paramedic. She learned that she had to undergo a lot of medical training and also be able to successfully deal with difficult and stressful situations. Paramedics have to be confident leaders who can quickly assess a situation, make decisions under pressure, and take action to stabilize a patient. They must remain calm, even in situations that may include violence or danger.

Sasha loved the outdoors and physical challenges, so after earning her certification, she went on to become a wilderness paramedic. She had dealt with wounds, burns, fractures, infections, heart attacks, and spinal cord injuries in the city, but that was with a well-equipped ambulance. Now, she had to learn to do similar things after being lowered by a helicopter into thick woods or onto a snowy mountain in extreme temperatures. She had to carry everything she needed, often pushing her body to its limits. During the difficult moments she remembered Manolo's words. *Somebody needs to do this work.* And like Manolo, Sasha knew that this job was her special destiny, and she excelled at it.

Finally— her first callout came as a wilderness medic! A hiker who had slipped off the trail and fallen onto a rocky ledge was conscious but couldn't move. As the helicopter approached the scene, Sasha's mind raced, but as she maneuvered down the rope to the injured hiker, she remained calm. She heard the man's friends screaming down from the trail and saw the panicked look on the hiker's face. Sasha knelt down and gave him her hand. "I'm here to help you; just stay calm," she whispered quietly in his ear. She knew she had the skills to keep that promise.

SLEUTH WORK

Ask Questions List three questions about wilderness medics you would be interested in researching. Where would you look to find information about this career?

Gather Evidence List clues in the text that show why Sasha wanted to become a wilderness medic.

Make Your Case Some people think that only those who are addicted to danger would take a high-risk job such as a wilderness medic. Do you agree or disagree? Use text evidence to help support your opinion.

Birthday Blues

Today was turning out to be one of the worst birthdays of Jacob's life. The trouble had started several days ago when his best friends—that is, the guys he had thought were his best friends—began shutting him out. One day Steven and Marco had gone to lunch without him, something that never happened, and when Jacob finally discovered where they were sitting, it was as if he'd caught two guilty conspirators in some kind of secret plot. Jacob had actually seen Steven laugh and whisper something to Marco when he thought that Jacob wasn't looking.

Jacob took it hard. He was completely perplexed. The boys had been friends, confidants, and teammates since T-ball days, and they never ignored or shut out one another. The three of them went everywhere together.

Today, things reached rock bottom when Jacob said he had some extra money and would buy everyone a slice of pizza before they went their separate ways home. "I can't," Marco shot back without even thinking about the offer. In fact, he hadn't even looked Jacob in the eye before running off.

"But it's my—" Jacob began before getting his second rejection, this one from Steven.

"Not today," Steven interrupted, glancing down nervously. Still not raising his eyes, Steven mumbled, "Uh, we've got that vocabulary test to study for."

That's when Jacob's face clouded, and he felt his stomach churning. Since when did Steven worry about vocabulary tests? Feeling lied to—and especially not wanting to embarrass himself— Jacob turned away quickly and went back to his locker. There he stood for several minutes, breathing deeply and shuffling papers until he was confident Steven and Marco were gone.

When he finally got home and noticed his aunt's car out front, Jacob's mood brightened a bit because he knew he could at least hang out with his cousins. After opening the door and laying his backpack down, balloons, streamers, and shouts of "Happy Birthday!" greeted him. He spotted a big cake sitting on the table before his mom and aunt smothered him with hugs. And then he noticed Steven and Marco standing off to the side with his cousins and a few neighborhood friends. Red-faced and smiling, they both looked as if they'd just pulled off the biggest surprise ever.

Sleuth Work

Gather Evidence List details in the text that tell why Jacob was upset by Steven's and Marco's behavior.

Ask Questions What questions would you ask a friend if the two of you were planning a surprise party?

Make Your Case Do you think that Steven and Marco deserve any criticism for how they acted? Were they good friends to Jacob throughout the story, or were they ever mean or unkind to him? Find at least three specific details from the text to explain and support your opinion.

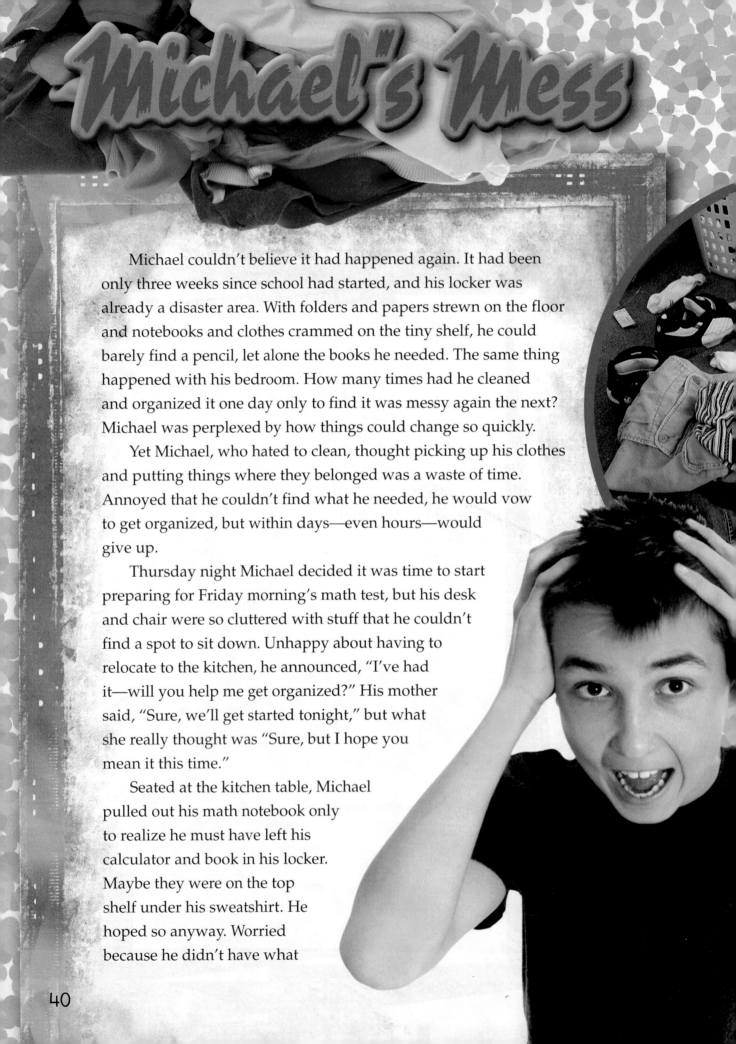

Michael's Mess

Michael couldn't believe it had happened again. It had been only three weeks since school had started, and his locker was already a disaster area. With folders and papers strewn on the floor and notebooks and clothes crammed on the tiny shelf, he could barely find a pencil, let alone the books he needed. The same thing happened with his bedroom. How many times had he cleaned and organized it one day only to find it was messy again the next? Michael was perplexed by how things could change so quickly.

Yet Michael, who hated to clean, thought picking up his clothes and putting things where they belonged was a waste of time. Annoyed that he couldn't find what he needed, he would vow to get organized, but within days—even hours—would give up.

Thursday night Michael decided it was time to start preparing for Friday morning's math test, but his desk and chair were so cluttered with stuff that he couldn't find a spot to sit down. Unhappy about having to relocate to the kitchen, he announced, "I've had it—will you help me get organized?" His mother said, "Sure, we'll get started tonight," but what she really thought was "Sure, but I hope you mean it this time."

Seated at the kitchen table, Michael pulled out his math notebook only to realize he must have left his calculator and book in his locker. Maybe they were on the top shelf under his sweatshirt. He hoped so anyway. Worried because he didn't have what

he needed to study, Michael went to bed, determined to get to his locker early the next morning.

When he awoke late on Friday, he panicked. In his messy room, he couldn't find the shirt he wanted to wear or his backpack—he couldn't even find matching socks. With every passing minute, as he rushed around throwing his stuff into a bag, he became more and more stressed.

By the time Michael arrived at school, only minutes remained before his first period class, math. He raced to his locker and began pawing through the clutter, looking for the missing calculator and book—but without success. When the first bell rang, he hurried to class in a frenzy, knowing that he was not well prepared for the test. He drew in a deep breath and quickly made a plan: he would concentrate on the exam and then he would get himself organized, finally.

Sleuth Work

Gather Evidence List at least three details that reveal how Michael was feeling on Thursday night.

Ask Questions Write three questions you would ask someone who wants your help in becoming more organized. How would answers to these questions be useful to you when helping that person?

Make Your Case Do you believe Michael has learned a lasting lesson? Will he be able to keep his room and locker organized for more than a short time? Justify your opinion by citing details from the text.

Unit 4
Explorers, Pioneers, and Discoverers

Howdy, Sleuthhounds!

In this unit, you will be looking for clues about some cool explorers, pioneers, and discoverers. Here are some sleuth tips to help you. Enjoy the ride!

Sleuth Tips

Gather Evidence

How do sleuths remember clues?

- Sleuths realize the importance of taking notes on the details. This helps them focus on finding new clues!
- Sleuths find different ways to record information: notes, lists, charts. They make sure not to lose valuable evidence.

Ask Questions

Why do sleuths ask questions?

- Sleuths know that you don't get great answers without great questions.
- Sleuths ask questions that help everyone think more deeply about the topic.

Make Your Case

How do sleuths work with other sleuths?

- Sleuths know what they think. However, they also want to know what others think about the same things.
- Sleuths understand that other sleuths may have reached different conclusions. They respect what others have to say.

Prove It!

What do sleuths think about before showing what they have learned?

- Sleuths prepare by reviewing their notes. They weed out irrelevant details. They focus on what is most important.
- Sleuths create a clear and convincing way to show what they have learned. They often make an outline of key points.

Surviving Against Odds

Throughout history, people have learned to survive in harsh conditions. The Bedouin (BED oo in) live in deserts of the Middle East and North Africa, some of the most inhospitable places in the world. They know from experience how to find fresh water in the dew on desert grass or under stones in the sand. For centuries, before the use of maps and compasses, the Bedouin followed tracks during the day and the North Star at night to find their way—often on camels—in the vast expanses of sand.

Far from the desert regions where the Bedouin live, modern outdoor adventurers can take courses in desert survival techniques. Trained survivalists or park rangers lead these hands-on programs. Most participants quickly recognize lack of water and extreme temperatures as the two main dangers. Instructors advise them how to find shade or build shelter to survive in high temperatures (up to 120°F). To obtain water, leaders demonstrate how to seal a plastic bag over a green plant. The plant's leaves produce moisture that then collects in the bag. As a last resort, crushing a cactus can produce enough water to quench one's thirst temporarily. Students learn how to prevent heat stroke during the day and ways to stay warm at night. They and their instructors watch out for desert hazards like poisonous plants, snakes, lizards, and scorpions.

Participants know that the course will end soon and they aren't really stranded. But why would anyone choose such a rigorous

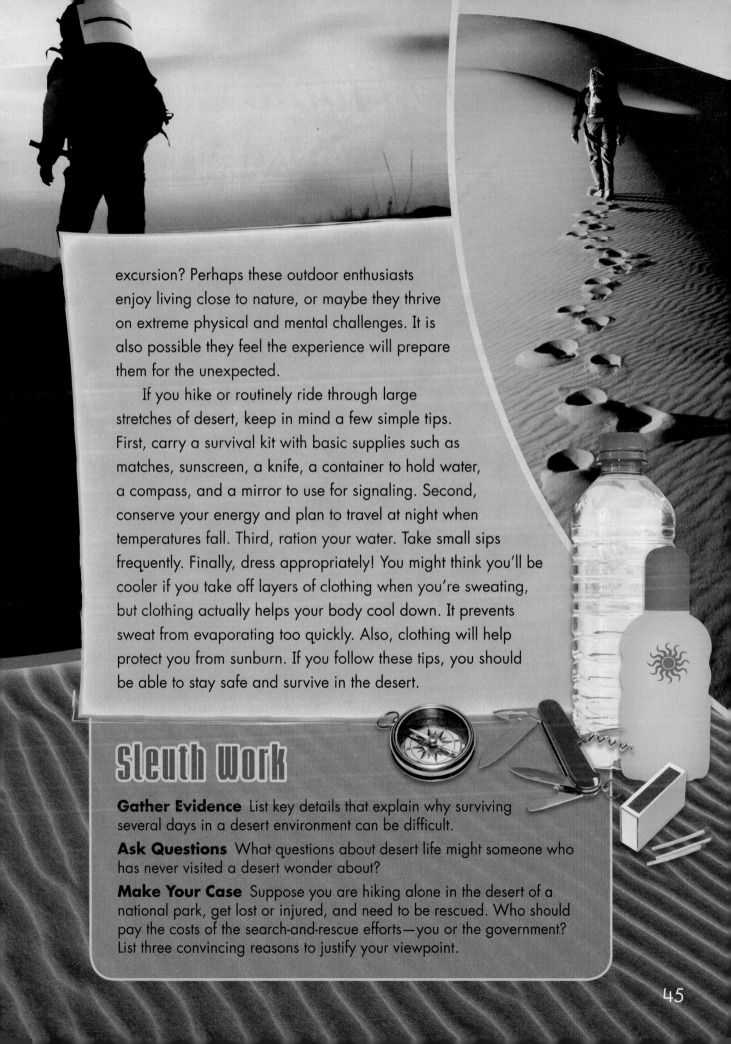

excursion? Perhaps these outdoor enthusiasts enjoy living close to nature, or maybe they thrive on extreme physical and mental challenges. It is also possible they feel the experience will prepare them for the unexpected.

If you hike or routinely ride through large stretches of desert, keep in mind a few simple tips. First, carry a survival kit with basic supplies such as matches, sunscreen, a knife, a container to hold water, a compass, and a mirror to use for signaling. Second, conserve your energy and plan to travel at night when temperatures fall. Third, ration your water. Take small sips frequently. Finally, dress appropriately! You might think you'll be cooler if you take off layers of clothing when you're sweating, but clothing actually helps your body cool down. It prevents sweat from evaporating too quickly. Also, clothing will help protect you from sunburn. If you follow these tips, you should be able to stay safe and survive in the desert.

Sleuth Work

Gather Evidence List key details that explain why surviving several days in a desert environment can be difficult.

Ask Questions What questions about desert life might someone who has never visited a desert wonder about?

Make Your Case Suppose you are hiking alone in the desert of a national park, get lost or injured, and need to be rescued. Who should pay the costs of the search-and-rescue efforts—you or the government? List three convincing reasons to justify your viewpoint.

A New Home
for KABANDA

Every morning when Olivia was hurrying to clean cages at the zoo's monkey house, she passed by the small elephant enclosure where Kabanda lived. Often, she heard him speaking to her as she passed. He typically made a soft rumbling sound that Olivia was certain meant "I'm lonely."

Olivia knew that elephants are very social animals, and Kabanda had been all alone in his enclosure for almost two years now, ever since his mate Adana had died. So, every morning, Olivia made sure she answered back in her most soothing voice, "I know, Kabanda, I know."

Some mornings Olivia would notice that Kabanda just swayed a little and bobbed his head. She knew this behavior was common in elephants held in captivity for long periods. She had read articles about how they began to show signs of sadness, even depression. Olivia would tell Kabanda, "So many people care about you. Change is coming, Kabanda!"

And it was. Olivia was not the only one who felt bad for the huge animal isolated in its tiny, cramped space. Kabanda had been in the news ever since his companion had died. The old zoo where he lived and Olivia worked had been built before people fully understood and sympathized with the needs of animals in captivity.

The elephant enclosure drew the most criticism because much of the public now believed that elephants needed vast natural expanses, with acres and acres of land. However, Kabanda was confined to a half-acre or so. Some zoo visitors interpreted the loud trumpeting sound Kabanda sometimes made as a cry of misery. Others said that there was no such thing as a good zoo for elephants. Elephants, they argued, needed entire wildlife parks, where several animal families could roam around and find their own food.

Kabanda never got the wildlife park, but his suffering at the old zoo didn't last much longer. One morning Olivia stopped at his enclosure, pointed west beyond the city boundaries, and said, "Kabanda, I have the best news for you. You're moving to a new zoo over that hill. It's much bigger, and best of all, there are other elephants. You will not be alone." Of course, Olivia knew that Kabanda couldn't understand what she was saying. But when the elephant suddenly lifted his head and trumpeted, Olivia wondered if maybe he understood her after all.

Sleuth Work

Gather Evidence Find clues that explain why Olivia felt Kabanda was unhappy.

Ask Questions Ask three questions about elephants in captivity that the story doesn't answer.

Make Your Case Some people believe animals should not be kept in zoos. Others support zoos for preservation and educational purposes. List three convincing reasons to support your viewpoint.

Bound for Kansas!

Jefferson Wilson was born into slavery in the South. The North's victory in the Civil War had promised opportunities for a better life, but the realities had fallen far short of what he expected. For all intents and purposes, as sharecroppers, Wilson and other former slaves were not truly free. No wonder they were dissatisfied with life in their Tennessee town.

A white man owned the land that Jefferson Wilson, his wife, and his three sons worked. The rent was so high and the rates for crops so low that his family was constantly in debt. The same was true for all sharecroppers. Living conditions were harsh, and racial tensions made Wilson worry for the safety of his family.

One day as he walked through Nashville, Jefferson Wilson spotted an advertisement for homesteading in Kansas. An acquaintance of his, businessman Benjamin Singleton, had posted it. Wilson investigated further and soon realized that he could afford transportation for his family if he didn't buy seeds for another year of sharecropping. After long discussions with friends and family—many of whom chose to stay in Tennessee—the Wilsons decided to head west with Mr. Singleton and one other family to help establish the all-black community of Dunlap, Kansas. The journey was long and difficult, with yellow fever claiming the lives of several travelers. Hopes of finding new opportunities sustained the pioneers.

When the Wilsons arrived, they faced many physical and emotional challenges. Farming the Kansas land proved difficult, and they were lonely. But one thing made all the difference—Jefferson Wilson and his neighbors owned the land they worked and the houses they built. It was theirs. Though they experienced some

Original advertisement encouraging homesteading in Kansas

Ho for Kansas!

Brethren, Friends, & Fellow Citizens:

I feel thankful to inform you that the

REAL ESTATE

AND

Homestead Association,

Will Leave Here the

15th of April, 1878,

In pursuit of Homes in the Southwestern Lands of America, at Transportation Rates, cheaper than ever was known before.

For full information inquire of

Benj. Singleton, better known as old Pap,

NO. 5 NORTH FRONT STREET.

Beware of Speculators and Adventurers, as it is a dangerous thing to fall in their hands.

Nashville, Tenn., March 18, 1878.

discrimination in Kansas, they no longer lived in constant fear for their lives.

The community established its own school—The Dunlap Academy and Mission School— which Wilson was proud to say his sons attended. As time passed, more and more people came to Dunlap, creating a tight-knit community of hundreds of black families.

Sleuth Work

Gather Evidence What motivated Jefferson Wilson to leave Tennessee for Kansas? List at least three clues from the story that help explain why he moved.

Ask Questions List three questions you would like to ask Jefferson Wilson or his family about their first year living in Dunlap, Kansas.

Make Your Case Imagine you were a neighbor of Jefferson Wilson and a sharecropper in Tennessee. Would you have decided to leave Tennessee for Dunlap, Kansas? Why or why not? Use details from the text to support your answer.

Despite the difficulties of constructing their sod house and clearing ground to plant, Jefferson Wilson and his wife never regretted their decision to begin a new life in Kansas. Eventually, their crops prospered, and life became easier. They had sacrificed a lot to start over, but they knew they had made the right choice for their family. Most importantly, they finally knew what freedom truly meant.

Underwater Explorer

By the middle of the twentieth century, it seemed that almost the entire world had been explored. Adventurers had visited Mount Everest, the South Pole, and the North Pole, along with the densest forests and the driest deserts Earth had to offer. It was not a great time for a person to try to make a name for himself as an explorer. But Jacques-Yves Cousteau (coo STOH) was not daunted by the fact that almost every spot on dry land had already been visited by someone. Instead, Cousteau made a name for himself by exploring what many considered the last frontier of Earth—the oceans.

Born in 1910 in France, Cousteau began his studies of the oceans around 1936. Over the next few years, he did a considerable amount of deep-sea diving; in 1943, he dove about 59 feet (18 meters) into the ocean and made a short film about what the world looked like that far underwater. A few years later, Cousteau helped develop better and more reliable gear for underwater travel, making it possible for adventurers—such as Cousteau himself—to spend more and more time underwater.

Between the 1950s and the 1970s, Cousteau carried out a number of studies involving the oceans and marine life. For example, he located shipwrecks and studied them closely. He also made some important discoveries regarding porpoises and their use of sonar to navigate. In addition, he spread a message of environmental awareness by encouraging people not to pollute the oceans.

Cousteau developed a variety of machines and vehicles that could travel deeper into the ocean. In 1956, for instance, he built a saucer-like vehicle that could reach 1,148 feet (350 meters) into the sea. A decade later he designed another one that traveled 1,640 feet (500 meters) below the surface. Throughout his time underwater, Cousteau filmed the undersea world and later shared the films with people across the world. His work greatly increased knowledge of the oceans and its life forms.

Through this work Cousteau became famous—and somewhat controversial. Several scientists charged that he was too interested in popularizing the world below the ocean

Jacques-Yves Cousteau

surface and not interested enough in studying it. Today some claim also that because Cousteau was not a trained oceanographer—a scientist who studies the ocean— he sometimes oversimplified scientific ideas in his books, films, and lectures. Despite this controversy, Cousteau remains well known today for his work. Cousteau died in 1997 after a long and adventure-filled life.

Gather Evidence Find information about Cousteau's accomplishments. List at least three ways he and his work influenced people's understanding and exploration of the oceans.

Ask Questions Look closely at the images that accompany this article. What questions do they raise that you would like to ask an oceanographer?

Make Your Case Do you think the U.S. government should increase the amount of money it spends each year on ocean research and exploration programs? Why or why not? List and explain at least two reasons to convince others that your opinion is correct.

Nature Copycats!

Twenty-first century inventions allow us to do things that once were thought to be science fiction. We launch people into space, replace worn-out or diseased body parts, and have immediate access to vast amounts of information on our phones. Humans are the greatest inventors on Earth, right? Well . . . maybe not.

An invention is a solution to a problem. Since the first bacteria appeared on this planet 3.8 billion years ago, the ability to solve problems has meant the difference between life and death for living organisms. Through adaptation, animals, plants, and microbes have found different ways to adapt to diverse environments on Earth. Today, scientists in the field of biomimicry focus on the natural world as the source of inspiration to solve human problems. *Biomimicry* comes from *bio-,* meaning "life," and *mimic,* meaning "to imitate." Consider, for example, how the Wright brothers' observations of flying birds inspired their design of early airplanes.

Here are several more recent examples to explore:

- Certain bacteria living in oil pipelines get energy and food by breaking down oil. Engineers now use these bacteria to clean pipelines and oil storage tanks and clean up oil spills.
- The structure of butterfly wings repels dirt and causes water to roll off of them. Engineers copy that structure when formulating dirt-resistant paints and textiles, including a well-known brand of jeans.
- Many species of winged insects use their panel-like wings to capture solar radiation and to move air in ways that produce remarkable flying ability. An innovative sailboat design mimics this technique to take advantage of wind and solar energy, the two most abundant and inexhaustible energy sources on Earth.
- Because their fibers are arranged in the direction of forces acting on them, tree trunks are resistant to breaking. For whom has this

Butterfly wings provide a model for dirt-resistant paints and textiles.

Bacteria clean oil pipelines.

discovery been useful? It has been especially useful to engineers who replicate this structure to build composite materials. Cars designed with these principles are as crash-safe as conventional cars, but up to 30 percent lighter.

- Biomimicry has produced many inventions that produce sustainable energy, such as the bioWAVE—units mounted to the ocean floor that convert wave motion to electricity. The way in which the units are attached to the sea floor and their ability to move and rotate to capture wave motion are modeled after seaweed.

Plants and animals have inspired thousands of other technologies. So, the next time you have a problem, you might ask: *How does nature solve it?*

Seaweed motion contributes to the development of sustainable energies.

Car design is inspired by the natural world.

A sailboat design mimics the wings of insects.

Sleuth Work

Gather Evidence Find evidence of at least two ways some inventions are inspired by nature.

Ask Questions Ask one question about the general field of biomimicry and one question about one of the specific technologies mentioned. Where would you look to answer those questions?

Make Your Case Would it be easier to study a natural solution and find a human problem it solves, or to start with a human problem and then find a solution based in nature? Cite text evidence to explain your reasoning and justify your viewpoint.

53

Unit 5
Resources

Hey there, Sleuthhounds!

In this unit, you will be looking for clues about resources. Here are some sleuth tips to help you. Check it out!

Sleuth Tips

Gather Evidence

How do sleuths find clues given by authors?

- Sleuths know that authors may include hints and clues in the text.

- Sleuths read and reread, looking for clues about sequence or cause and effect. These hints can lead to important evidence.

Ask Questions

Where do sleuths get answers to their questions?

- Sleuths look everywhere in the text and images for answers. They share what they know with other sleuths.

- Sleuths do research on computers and in books. They know that some questions may take a lifetime to answer.

Make Your Case

How do sleuths use evidence when they make a case?

- Sleuths explain their ideas and thinking by presenting evidence and then explaining how they reached their conclusions.

- Sleuths cite where they found the text or visual evidence. They know that explaining where evidence came from is important.

Prove It!

Why do sleuths think about who will read what they write?

- Sleuths know how to write in a variety of formats and styles. They understand that their writing should always be clear.

- Sleuths are skillful and can determine the best way to present what they have learned. They use texts, models, and diagrams.

The Hat Man

The first day, when Mr. Hatton had helped out in reading corner, the four-year-olds had yawned and squirmed in response to his soft, slow voice. The second day, when he had sat at the art table, he couldn't think of anything to paint. Volunteering at a nursery school wasn't turning out quite as he'd thought it would. In fact, it was turning out to be as challenging as pulling a rabbit out of a hat.

Today Ms. Chen, the lead teacher, had assigned him to imaginative play. Feeling glum, Mr. Hatton didn't know how he was going to amuse the fidgety four-year-olds. Indeed, he was thinking to himself, "I'm too old to be trying to relate to these little ones" when he spotted a pile of dress-up clothes. It was the hats in that pile that told him that maybe he could accommodate his audience and enjoy himself, too.

Gathering the children around him, he announced excitedly that they would play a mystery guessing game called "What's My Hat?" He would pretend to be someone, and when the children guessed who he was, they could find the right hat and put it on his head.

First, Mr. Hatton said *clip clop, clip clop* and neighed as he marched around the children. All the while he moved his body up and down as if he were galloping on a horse. As he swung an imaginary rope over his head, Helene ran for the cowboy hat. Mr. Hatton bowed low enough for her to place the hat on his head, all the while neighing. Then he removed the hat, twirled around with a flourish to signal he was starting over, and wailed like a fire engine siren. As he did so, he pantomimed pointing a squirting hose at a burning building. This time it was Diego who grabbed the right hat and, with a smile, placed it on Mr. Hatton's head.

The children were engaged, eagerly crowding around him as he made silly sounds and pantomimed clues that drew forth the police officer's cap, the pirate's hat, the queen's crown, the bike rider's helmet, and the construction worker's hard hat. Nobody—not even Mr. Hatton himself—wanted to stop playing when snack time came. In fact, for many days later, Helene was calling Mr. Hatton "Mr. Hat Man," and Mr. Hatton was satisfied with the new hat he was wearing in life.

Sleuth Work

Gather Evidence Find details that show why Mr. Hatton was pleased to notice the hats in the pile of dress-up clothes.

Ask Questions What else would you like to know about Mr. Hatton's volunteer work? List three questions that the story does not answer about his experiences at the nursery school.

Make Your Case Who do you think learned more from playing "What's My Hat?" Mr. Hatton or the children? Use details from the story to explain your conclusion.

Eulogy for Dr. Dorothy Height
by President Barack Obama

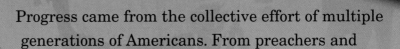

Below is an excerpt from a eulogy that President Barack Obama delivered in honor of educator and social activist Dr. Dorothy Height on April 29, 2010, praising her life and describing it as "a life that lifted other lives; a life that changed this country for the better over the course of nearly one century here on Earth."

Progress came from the collective effort of multiple generations of Americans. From preachers and lawyers, and thinkers and doers, men and women like Dr. Height, who took it upon themselves—often at great risk—to change this country for the better. . . .

Well, Dr. Dorothy Height deserves a place in this pantheon. She, too, deserves a place in our history books. She, too, deserves a place of honor in America's memory.

Look at her body of work. Desegregating the YWCA. Laying the groundwork for integration on Wednesdays in Mississippi. Lending pigs to poor farmers as a sustainable source of income. Strategizing with civil rights leaders, holding her own, the only woman in the room, Queen Esther to this Moses Generation—even as she led the National Council of Negro Women with vision and energy—with vision and energy, vision and class.

But we remember her not solely for all she did during the civil rights movement.

We remember her for all she did over a lifetime, behind the scenes, to broaden the movement's reach. To shine a light on stable families and tight-knit communities. To make us see the drive for civil rights and women's rights not as a separate struggle, but as part of a larger movement to secure the rights of all humanity, regardless of gender, regardless of race, regardless of ethnicity.

It's an unambiguous record of righteous work, worthy of remembrance, worthy of recognition. And yet, one of the ironies is, is that year after year, decade in, decade out, Dr. Height went about her work quietly, without fanfare, without self-promotion. She never cared about who got the credit. She didn't need to see her picture in the papers. She understood that the movement gathered strength from the bottom up, those unheralded men and women who don't always make it into the history books but who steadily insisted on their dignity, on their manhood and womanhood. She wasn't interested in credit. What she cared about was the cause. The cause of justice. The cause of equality. The cause of opportunity.

Sleuth Work

Ask Questions List three factual questions you would like to research about Dr. Dorothy Height's life.

Gather Evidence Why did Dr. Height deserve to be honored? Identify at least three important accomplishments of hers that the eulogy specifically mentions.

Make Your Case Did everyone in America benefit from Dr. Height's work, or did one group benefit more than others? List two reasons to support your answer.

Tornado Alley

The first week of May in Tornado Alley was particularly active that year. Nearly every day after school, Kristen heard the tornado siren from the nearby Oklahoma town, stopped whatever she was doing, and hurried to the protection of the basement with her family.

It just so happened that Kristen's best friend, Julia, who had never spent an entire tornado season in the area, was staying with Kristen because Julia's parents were both traveling for business. As the girls chatted in the yard, the tornado siren wailed. Kristen stopped in mid-sentence and turned toward the house. Looking puzzled, Julia asked what Kristen was doing. "Going to the basement—what else would I be doing with that siren blaring?"

Julia stared at Kristen as if she were crazy and explained that neither she nor her parents were worried when the siren went off. In fact, they often sat on the front porch to watch the oncoming storm. Just then, Kristen saw her mom waving from the porch, grabbed Julia's arm, and scurried toward the house.

Once in the basement, Kristen told her mom what Julia and her family usually did when they heard the sirens. Kristen's mom said, "Julia, let me tell you just how serious these tornado sirens are. This house you are sitting in is not the same house we bought— the original was destroyed by a tornado while we were huddling together in this very basement."

Julia's heart began to race as Kristen's mother continued. "That tornado had estimated winds of nearly 165 miles per hour, rating it an EF-3. That means it was rated severe on the Enhanced Fujita (foo-JEE-ta) Scale. Are you familiar with tornado ratings?"

Julia nodded, replying that she had learned about the Fujita Scale in science and knew that it classified tornados by the damage they had done.

Enhanced Fujita Scale

Rating	Wind Speed	Damage
EF-0	65–85 mph	Minor
EF-1	86–110 mph	Moderate
EF-2	111–135 mph	Considerable
EF-3	136–165 mph	Severe
EF-4	166–200 mph	Extreme
EF-5	Over 200 mph	Catastrophic

Kristen's mom continued, "I have never been so terrified in my entire life! I was so grateful to have made it through unscathed." In a low, firm voice, she described how the tornado sounded like a rumbling freight train, how the house shook violently, how they could hear the walls collapsing upstairs, and finally how one person in the community had died. By the time she had finished, Julia's face was pale, her eyes teary, and her expression solemn. She wished her parents were home; she had a lot to talk to them about.

Sleuth Work

Ask Questions List three questions about tornados or tornado warning sirens you would like to ask an extreme weather expert.

Gather Evidence Why should tornado warnings be taken seriously? Use information in the text to identify three convincing reasons.

Make Your Case Do you think that it was fortunate or unfortunate for Julia that both of her parents had to be out of town during the day the story describes? Use details from the text to explain your answer.

Blue Gold!

   Did you know that the denim jeans you are wearing or have in your closet might have been called "Jacob's" instead of "Levi's"? The story of how two hardworking and creative immigrants came together to produce the first blue jeans—that icon of American style—is more interesting than you might think.

   In 1848, a young German named Loeb Strauss immigrated to New York with his mother and two sisters. His older brothers owned a company that sold fabric and clothing there. After gold was discovered in California, Strauss saw it as a business opportunity. Gold was a valuable resource, but while some gold prospectors "struck it rich," many other people grew wealthy providing the more mundane goods and services that miners and other California settlers needed. In 1853, young Strauss, now called Levi, traveled to California and began distributing his brothers' fabric and clothing.

   Contrary to popular myth, however, Levi Strauss did not invent the blue jeans known as "Levi's." Born in Latvia (LAT-vee-uh), Jacob Davis was a tailor who made clothing and utilitarian items like horse blankets. As the demand for heavy-duty work clothes grew, Davis, who lived in Nevada, began making "waist-high overalls" from cotton duck, which is like canvas. He purchased the cotton duck from Strauss. The term blue jeans comes from a fabric called "jean" that is much like denim and was used for pants in the nineteenth century.

   Because thread alone wasn't strong enough to fasten the pockets onto the pants, Jacob decided to add copper rivets, which he had successfully used on horse blankets. As the durable pants became more popular with miners, ranchers, and farmers, Davis decided to obtain a patent. In 1872, he wrote to Strauss, offering to share the rights to the riveting process if Strauss would help mass market the product.

   Strauss then brought Davis to San Francisco to supervise the manufacture of riveted jeans by Levi Strauss & Co. On May 20, 1873, the patent was granted; in fact, that day is considered the official birthday of blue jeans. The pants soon became a best seller. Strauss and Davis had struck "blue gold."

Levi Strauss

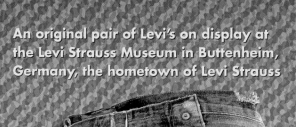

An original pair of Levi's on display at the Levi Strauss Museum in Buttenheim, Germany, the hometown of Levi Strauss

Rivets are still used today in the manufacturing of Levi's.

An advertisement from about 1874 for Levi's jeans

Sleuth Work

Ask Questions List two questions about Levi Strauss, Jacob Davis, or their partnership that you would be interested to research.

Gather Evidence List several key characteristics of the "waist-high overalls" Jacob Davis made.

Make Your Case Blue jeans were invented in the mid-nineteenth century for miners, ranchers, and others doing heavy, strenuous work. Why do you think the jeans remain so popular today? List text details that help explain and support your conclusion.

Shaping Tomorrow Through Innovation Today

Suppose you could fast forward to the year 2075. Has the world run out of gasoline and clean water, or has new technology conserved important resources? If we adapt now to energy-efficient lifestyles and products, life in the future will be better than it is today. Many smart changes are already in the works.

To decrease air pollution and gas consumption, cities are encouraging people to ride bicycles. The Boston Bikes program has doubled the number of bicycle riders by adding bike routes and places to park bikes. New York City has announced plans for a bike-share program. After adding 250 miles of bike paths, the city is purchasing bicycles and developing rental stations. However, objections to the location of stations still must be resolved.

Automobile manufacturers are producing electric cars that travel farther between charges, making them a practical replacement for gasoline-powered cars. With a recent invention of lithium-air batteries that use graphene bubbles, a car can go 300 miles on a single charge. In addition, one automaker is planning to introduce laser headlights that will be 1,000 times brighter than LED headlights yet use half the power. The amount of power needed to run the engine is reduced, but will the bright lights be safe? Engineers say yes.

Advances in solar and wind power are reducing our need for limited resources such as coal and oil.

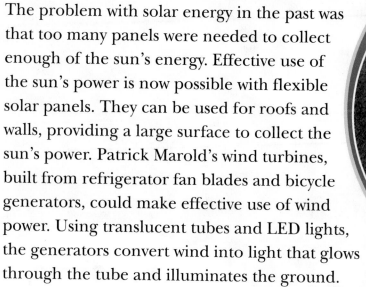

The problem with solar energy in the past was that too many panels were needed to collect enough of the sun's energy. Effective use of the sun's power is now possible with flexible solar panels. They can be used for roofs and walls, providing a large surface to collect the sun's power. Patrick Marold's wind turbines, built from refrigerator fan blades and bicycle generators, could make effective use of wind power. Using translucent tubes and LED lights, the generators convert wind into light that glows through the tube and illuminates the ground.

Another promising invention includes a fabric made from milk that feels like silk and is washable. Created by fashion designer Anke Domaske, Qmilch is environmentally friendly because it uses only a half-gallon of water to make 2 pounds of fabric, while more than 10,000 liters of water are needed for 2 pounds of cotton. Changing our lives today will make the year 2075 a wonderful time to be alive.

Sleuth Work

Gather Evidence Find clues that show the writer's belief that changes in lifestyles and new products will lead to better lives in the future.

Ask Questions List three questions an expert looking at the future might want to study more closely. What are two questions or concerns people looking at energy-efficient products might have?

Make Your Case Draw a conclusion about life in 2075. Is the writer's claim about innovations a realistic solution to the problem of limited resources? Give three reasons to support your viewpoint.

Unit 6
Exploring Cultures

Welcome, Sleuthhounds!
In this unit, you will be looking for clues to exploring other cultures. Here are some sleuth tips to help you. Enjoy the adventure!

Sleuth Tips

Gather Evidence

How do sleuths know if evidence is important?

- Sleuths keep track of clues and evidence. They don't necessarily know which ones will lead to answers.
- Sleuths examine the evidence closely and figure out which parts best connect to the answers they seek.

Ask Questions

How do sleuths think of interesting questions to ask?

- Sleuths take the creative route to asking questions. Super sleuths try to think of questions that are unique.
- Sleuths can find the missing pieces and ask questions to complete the puzzle.

Make Your Case

How do sleuths learn from other sleuths?

- Sleuths can learn a lot by listening to other sleuths. They might uncover some needed information.
- Sleuths find ways to gather new evidence by asking other sleuths questions.

Prove It!

How do sleuths prepare to share what they know?

- Sleuths rehearse and reread. They make any necessary changes to clarify their presentations.
- Sleuths know that practice makes perfect. They know the practice will pay off and allow them to enjoy the ride!

Cinderella—
What *Really* Happened

The other day on the bus when I saw a woman reading a book of fairy tales, I wanted to grab it from her and throw it out the window. Of all the pointless things to read, fairy tales have to rank at the top of the list. They're preachy and unreliable—in fact, half of them are complete lies. Take the story of Cinderella.

Look, ever since high school, I've been friends with Cinderella's older stepsister. Anyone who reads that story gets all *oh, Cinderella was soooo nice and sweet* and *oh, those stepsisters were soooo horrible,* but that's all wrong. See, I was there, and I know the girls were all treated equally. I hate to break it to you, but the truth is that Cindy—well, she's always been a spoiled brat and a total drama queen.

Although she says she was mistreated, that simply isn't true. Now I don't like to say nasty things about anyone, so let's just say Cindy broke the rules, *a lot.* I can't even count the times she missed her curfew or ignored her chores. While I was helping her stepsisters clean the house, she would lie around reading fashion magazines, giving her precious little feet a pedicure or chattering incessantly about marrying a rich guy. That girl was so superficial—and talk about a bad attitude.

As for being forbidden to go to the prince's ball, well, that's true, but it certainly isn't the whole story. Truth is, she'd been invited to the ball—we all were—and her stepmother even bought her this gorgeous gown. But Cindy's last report card had been just terrible, plus she lied about it, so naturally her parents had grounded her. That's the *only* reason why she had to stay home that evening.

Only what happened then was that she sneaked out of the house to go to the ball anyway. And next thing you know, Cindy's marrying the prince and becoming the queen. She's hiring publicists to write stories about how terrific she is and how badly her stepsisters and stepmother treated her. You know, come to think of it, maybe I should sell my story to a tabloid or something—

Anyway, you know how they say that in fairy tales the good characters get rewarded and the bad ones get punished? Well, you shouldn't believe everything you read.

Sleuth Work

Gather Evidence List evidence from the story that shows that the narrator dislikes Cinderella.

Ask Questions What more would you like to know about the narrator? List one question you would like to ask her and one question you would like to ask an adult who knows her well.

Make Your Case How much do you think the narrator can be trusted? Explain your viewpoint, giving evidence from the text to support your case.

IT'S ALL GREEK TO US!

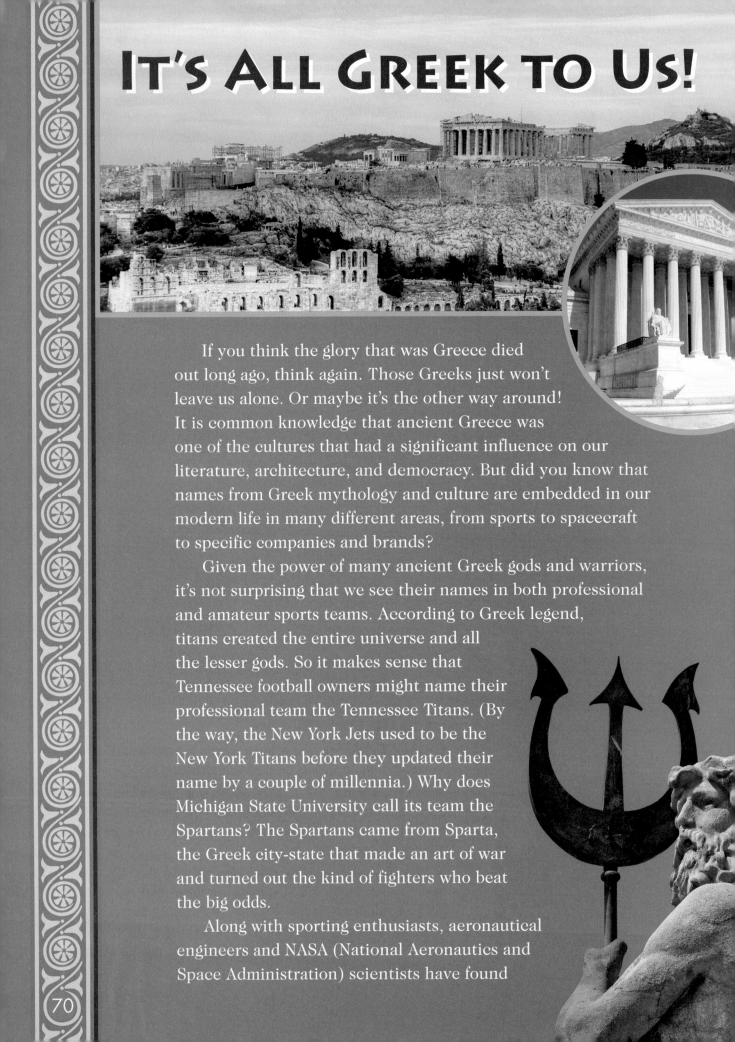

If you think the glory that was Greece died out long ago, think again. Those Greeks just won't leave us alone. Or maybe it's the other way around! It is common knowledge that ancient Greece was one of the cultures that had a significant influence on our literature, architecture, and democracy. But did you know that names from Greek mythology and culture are embedded in our modern life in many different areas, from sports to spacecraft to specific companies and brands?

Given the power of many ancient Greek gods and warriors, it's not surprising that we see their names in both professional and amateur sports teams. According to Greek legend, titans created the entire universe and all the lesser gods. So it makes sense that Tennessee football owners might name their professional team the Tennessee Titans. (By the way, the New York Jets used to be the New York Titans before they updated their name by a couple of millennia.) Why does Michigan State University call its team the Spartans? The Spartans came from Sparta, the Greek city-state that made an art of war and turned out the kind of fighters who beat the big odds.

Along with sporting enthusiasts, aeronautical engineers and NASA (National Aeronautics and Space Administration) scientists have found inspiration for names in Greek mythology. For example, the Apollo space mission was named after the god of the sun, who drove his chariot across the sky. The Gemini program was named after a pair of mythological twins. And then there are the Poseidon and Trident missiles, named after the Greek god of the sea and his three-pronged spear. The military folks who gave the name Hercules to a series of large transport aircraft likely had the legendary Greek strongman in mind.

Crew for the *Apollo 17* lunar landing mission

You might be familiar with an online store named after the mighty Amazon River. The Spanish explorers who named that river probably had heard of a group of powerful women warriors from Greek mythology called Amazons. You may have also heard of the moving company named after Atlas, the god who carried the world on his back.

Do a little investigating. You may be surprised to discover many products and businesses named for figures in Greek mythology. Figures such as Ajax, Orion, Oracle, Pandora, and Midas have new meanings to us today. Greeks are everywhere!

SLEUTH WORK

Gather Evidence List two examples from the text of sports teams that are named for figures in Greek mythology.

Ask Questions What are you curious about after reading this article? List two questions you would like to research.

Make Your Case Are the names drawn from Greek mythology and culture mentioned in this article still effective today? Refer to specific examples in the text as you explain your opinion.

THE FESTIVAL

Jose Fernandez immigrated with his family to the United States when he was three years old. By the time he reached sixth grade, his only noticeably Latino characteristics were his name and a bit of Spanish he spoke when his grandmother visited from Puerto Rico each year. Jose had never visited Puerto Rico. He knew little of his family's roots.

That partly explains why he wasn't excited about the news that his school was going to organize a multicultural festival for the first Saturday in March. "Boring!" Jose muttered as the school principal explained the festival. He said he needed students to organize booths for different countries. "So there will be three or four booths in the gym," Jose thought, "but what will we do there for a whole day?"

"Students, this will be a fun project," the principal declared, "and I think you all will learn a lot."

Then Mr. Li, the sixth-grade teacher, started explaining that the booths could include food, music, and crafts from each country. Jose's interest grew. As everyone began making plans, students began to talk about different cultures and origins. Patrick volunteered to organize the Ireland booth, while Daryl announced that his father moved here from Kenya. Cheena's family was from Northern India, and Katuk was from Bali. The enthusiasm that Jose's classmates had for their own cultures was contagious. "I can run the booth for Puerto Rico!" Jose interjected with a newfound excitement.

When Jose came home, he asked his dad if he could call his grandmother to get ideas for the booth. His dad agreed, but he also volunteered to help Jose himself.

"You know," he said, "I grew up in Puerto Rico, so I know a lot about the culture and the history. So does

your mom." Jose nodded eagerly when his dad suggested going through old family recipes to find something to cook for the festival.

Over the next month, Jose worked hard making posters and maps and gathering materials for his booth. Of all the booths, his was one of the most interesting and interactive. Jose beamed as everyone sampled the guava pudding, listened to salsa music, and shook the maracas he and his dad had made from gourds. The principal had been right. The festival had been a lot of fun. Jose had learned about different cultures, and perhaps more importantly about his own.

SLEUTH WORK

Ask Questions Suppose you were to write an article for the school newspaper about the multicultural festival. For your article, interview students about their experiences at the festival. List three questions you would like to ask them.

Gather Evidence What clues in the story help explain why Jose became excited about participating in the multicultural festival?

Make Your Case Is our nation's diversity or our nation's unity the greater strength? Provide three convincing reasons for your opinion.

Melting Pot or Salad Bowl?

How would you feel if your family decided to move to China, Egypt, or Spain? You might not speak the language, and the food would be different from what you're used to. You'd be in for a very different cultural experience. Would you expect teachers in your new school to speak English? Or would you need to learn the language and customs as fast as possible?

With the exception of Native Americans, every person living in the United States can trace his or her ancestry back to a different country. In our current population, about 12.5% of Americans were born in other countries. Some would argue that people who come here should adapt to the customs and language of the country. In the early twentieth century, Israel Zangwill wrote a play called *The Melting Pot*. In it, he likened America to a melting pot. He suggested that immigrants are blended together and transformed into "Americans."

Many have disagreed with that view, however, including former New York Representative Shirley Chisholm. "We are nobody's melting pot!" Chisholm said. "We are a beautiful, giant salad bowl." In Chisholm's view, the character and strength of America lies in the unique contributions of people from many different racial, ethnic, and cultural groups. In the "salad bowl" analogy, each ingredient (people of a different culture) retains its own identity.

So, how can a person stay true to his or her heritage and still be "American"? To what extent can and should schools promote "multiculturalism," encouraging the roles of various racial, ethnic, and cultural groups in society? For example, Muslim students are expected to pray five times daily no matter where they are. What should schools do about this? Should the school cafeteria take into account religious and cultural food restrictions? Should the dress code allow for cultural differences? Should teachers be required to teach in several languages?

Educators, politicians, and philosophers, as well as parents and students, find themselves debating these questions. Fear and prejudice and an "us versus them" mentality occur when different groups don't understand one another. Schools would seem to be an ideal place to get to know people from other cultures and to begin to think "internationally" rather than clinging to one's own "group." What do you think? How should schools encourage students to focus on what people have in common while still valuing and respecting their differences?

Sleuth Work

Gather Evidence Use information in the text to explain, in your own words, what it means to say American society is a "salad bowl" or a "melting pot."

Ask Questions List three questions you would like to research about how U.S. schools are adapting to ethnic, cultural, and religious differences among students.

Make Your Case What can or should a school do to address the increasing cultural and ethnic differences in the American population? Include at least two text details to explain and support your conclusion.

Taking Care of Immigrants: The Kohler Company

If you check out a bathroom sink or bathtub, you might see the name *Kohler* on it. In the late nineteenth century, John Michael Kohler, an immigrant from Austria, started the Kohler Company in Sheboygan, Wisconsin. Known for the high-quality bath and plumbing fixtures it manufactured, the business grew quickly. Among its most popular products were enameled bathtubs modeled after troughs used by farm animals! When the Sheboygan factory became too small, a new factory was built in a rural setting four miles away. By 1905, after the death of John Michael Kohler and two of his sons, another son, Walter, took charge. Under his leadership, the Kohler Company continued its commitment to improving the lives of its employees, many of whom were Austrian immigrants.

The Kohler Company emphasized worker safety, provided medical care, and offered above-average wages. All this contrasted sharply with other businesses throughout the Midwest that often exploited immigrant laborers. One of Walter Kohler's priorities was to ensure that Kohler employees not only had pleasant working conditions but also pleasant living conditions. For example, he did not want the growing village around the factory to become an overcrowded, ugly, industrial city. Kohler had been inspired by several

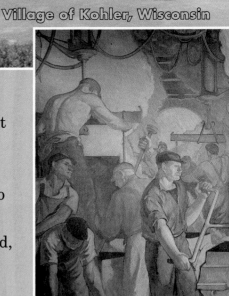

John Michael Kohler

Village of Kohler, Wisconsin

Kohler Company workers, 1889

Walter Kohler

planned cities he had toured throughout the United States and Europe. After consulting with top-notch architects, city planners, and landscape architects, he began transforming the Village of Kohler into one of the first planned communities in the Midwest.

The town had many attractive features: green spaces, single and two-family homes, recreational facilities, and a school. Creating a company town helped the Kohler business attract and retain a stable workforce, but it also provided employee benefits to employees. Under Walter Kohler's leadership, the company built the American Club, a dormitory for immigrant employees. Housing costs were minimal. Workers frequently paid less than $30 a month for room, board, and laundry. Many unmarried Kohler employees stayed there until they saved enough to buy a house and send for their families. Employees took lessons in English, American history, and civics. Immigrant workers got a day off and transportation to the courthouse as a first step toward becoming citizens.

When the American Club was dedicated in 1918, a company newsletter described it as a "building dedicated to democracy." Between 1900 and 1930, the Kohler Company helped at least 1,200 immigrant workers become citizens. As a biographer of Walter Kohler concluded, the American Club was truly an "Americanization Club."

Sleuth Work

Gather Evidence List at least three pieces of evidence that show how the Kohler Company tried to make life better for its immigrant employees.

Ask Questions What questions about the Village of Kohler or the American Club would you like to research further?

Make Your Case Do you think there are more advantages or more disadvantages for the employees of a company to live in company-owned housing? Explain your reasoning.

Acknowledgments

Photographs

Every effort has been made to secure permission and provide appropriate credit for photographic material. The publisher deeply regrets any omission and pledges to correct errors called to its attention in subsequent editions.

Unless otherwise acknowledged, all photographs are the property of Pearson Education, Inc.

Photo locators denoted as follows: Top (T), Center (C), Bottom (B), Left (L), Right (R), Background (Bkgd)

Cover

Chandler Digital Art

4 (TC) ©bejim/Fotolia, (Bkgrd) ©Nightman1965/Fotolia, (R) ©tungphoto/Fotolia, (TL) ©Zedcor Wholly Owned/Thinkstock, (TR) Maxx-Studio/Shutterstock, (BC) Shutterstock, (BL) taelove7/Shutterstock; **5** (TR) ©phant/Fotolia, (B) Hemera Technologies/Thinkstock; **8** (Bkgrd) ©Getty Images/Thinkstock, (T) ©Magnum/Fotolia, (BL) B.G. Smith/Shutterstock, (C) Iwona Grodzka/Shutterstock; **9** (TR) Shutterstock; **10** (BC) ©Rob/Fotolia; **11** (B) Shutterstock; **12** (Bkgrd) ©kenzo/Fotolia, (BL) ©rgbspace/Fotolia; **13** (TR) ©Craig Jewell/Fotolia, (BR) ©dzain/Fotolia; **14** (BL) ©popstock/Fotolia, (TC) ©UryadnikovS/Fotolia; **15** (Bkgrd) ©UryadnikovS/Fotolia; **16** (C) ©Jupiterimages/Thinkstock, (Bkgrd) ©lunamarina/Fotolia, (BL) ©martin1985/Fotolia; **17** (CR) ©Stephen Meese/Fotolia; **20** (C) Ablestock /Thinkstock, (Bkgrd) NASA; **21** (TR) Bill Ingalls/NASA; **22** (Bkgrd) ©DK Images, (TL) ©LPP/Fotolia, (CL) Brand X Pictures/Thinkstock; **23** (R) ©labelverte/Fotolia; **24** (Bkgrd) ©National Geographic Image Collection/Alamy Images; **26** (C) ©Arunas Gabalis/Fotolia, (C) ©Henrik Lehnerer/Shutterstock, (TL) ©picsfive/Fotolia; **27** (TR) ©DK Images, (B) NASA; **28** (T, L, BL) ©DK Images, (Bkgrd) ©Hemera Technologies/Thinkstock; **29** (BL) ©DK Images; **32** (Bkgrd) ©Composer/Fotolia, (BL) ©Delphimages/Fotolia; **33** (BC) ©benuch/Fotolia, (TR) ©Galyna Andrushko/Fotolia, (R) ©hmartin/Fotolia, (BR) ©pablo_hernan/Fotolia; **34** (B) ©Natis/Fotolia, (TL) Prints & Photographs Division, Library of Congress, (Bkgrd) Thinkstock; **36** (TL) ©Spid1981/Fotolia; **37** (BL) ©Monkey Business/Fotolia; **38** (T) ©Dmitry Koksharov/Fotolia, (Bkgrd) ©Ioana Davies/Fotolia, (B) MonkeyBusiness/Fotolia; **39** (CR) ©Lisa F. Young/Fotolia; **40** (T) ©kk/Fotolia, (Bkgrd) ©Lizard/Fotolia, (C) Adam Tinney/Shutterstock, (C) Leah-Anne Thompson/Shutterstock; **41** (BR) ©Le Do/Fotolia; **44** (Bkgrd) ©Galyna Andrushko/Fotolia, (BL) ©Kamila Panasiuk/Fotolia; **45** (R) ©Alexander Petrov/Fotolia, (R) ©Anne Del Socorro/Fotolia, (TR) ©Galyna Andrushko/Fotolia, (R) ©haveseen/Fotolia, (R) ©kmit/Fotolia, (R) ©Lucky Dragon/Fotolia; **46** (T) Shutterstock; **47** (BR) ©macdivers/Fotolia; **48** (B) ©Everett Collection Inc/Alamy Images, (Bkgrd) ©Ryan McVay/Thinkstock; **49** (T) Library of Congress, Prints & Photographs Division, HABS [or HAER or HALS], Reproduction number [e.g., "HABS ILL, 16-CHIG, 33-2 "]/Prints & Photographs Division, Library of Congress; **50** (TR) NASA; **51** (BR) ©John Anderson/Fotolia, (B) ©Paul Shawcross/Alamy Images; **52** (C) ©Danys Prykchodov/Fotolia, (Bkgrd) ©Iakov Kalinin/Fotolia, (T) ©John D. Simmons KRT/NewsCom, (T) ©Neo Edmund/Fotolia, (B) SolarSailor; **53** (TR) ©Kelpfish/Fotolia, (CR) ©lassedesignen/Fotolia; **56** (C) ©Gabees/Fotolia, (C) ©supertrooper/Fotolia, (C) ©vencav/Fotolia, (C) ©xtremer/Fotolia, (C) Comstock/Thinkstock, (T) Hemera Technologies/Thinkstock, (C) Stockbyte/Thinkstock, (Bkgrd) Thinkstock; **57** (BR) Digital Vision/Thinkstock; **58** (Bkgrd) ©LC-DIG-ppmsca-03128/Prints & Photographs Division, Library of Congress, (BL) ©TJ2 WENN Photos/NewsCom, (TR) Pete Souza/Prints & Photographs Division, Library of Congress; **59** (R) Warren K.Leffler/Prints & Photographs Division, Library of Congress; **60** (Bkgrd) ©Zastol'skiy Victor Leonidovich/Shutterstock; **61** (BR) Shutterstock; **62** (C) ©Pictorial Press Ltd/Alamy Images; **63** (L) ©A3609 Daniel Karmann Deutsche Presse-Agentur/NewsCom, (TR) ©Karmousha/Fotolia, (CR) ©Pictorial Press Ltd/Alamy Images; **64** (T) ©iNNOCENt/Fotolia, (BL) ©lassedesignen/Fotolia; **65** (BR) ©Julian Stratenschulte/DPA/ABACA/NewsCom, (TR) ©Lyroky/Alamy Images; **68** (L) ©Duey/Fotolia, (B) ©Olga Drabovich/Fotolia, (Bkgrd) ©red2000/Fotolia, (B) ©travis manley/Fotolia, (TL) Hemera Technologies/Thinkstock; **69** (T) ©Kirill Bodrov /Fotolia, (TR) ©ksena32/Fotolia, (BR) ©Loraliu/Fotolia; **70** (B) ©bbourdages/Fotolia, (C) ©Gary Blakeley/Fotolia, (Bkgrd) ©Leshik/Fotolia, (T) ©Stefanos Kyriazis/Fotolia; **71** (C) ©Dmitry Erashov/Fotolia, (BR) ©urbanhearts/Fotolia, (TR) NASA; **72** (C) ©aberenyi/Fotolia, (L) ©Andy Dean/Fotolia, (BL) Hemera Technologies/Thinkstock, (B) medioimages/Photodisc/Thinkstock; **73** (R) ©Jupiterimages/Thinkstock, (C) ©Monart Design/Fotolia, (BR) Thinkstock; **74** (BC) ©Katrina Brown/Fotolia, (BL) ©Yuri Arcurs/Fotolia; **75** (TR) ©Jasmin Merdan/Fotolia, (BR) ©Thomas Perkins/Fotolia; **76** (Bkgrd) ©Ryan McVay/Thinkstock, (C, B) Kohler Co.; **77** (T) Kohler Co..

Follow the path to close reading using the Super Sleuth Tips . . .

- Gather Evidence
- Ask Questions
- Make Your Case
- Prove It!

ISBN-13: 978-0-328-73059-9
ISBN-10:   0-328-73059-9

90000>

EAN

9 780328 730599

For Exams Scheduled After December 31, 2018

CPA EXAM REVIEW

FINAL REVIEW

BUSINESS

BECKER

PROFESSIONAL EDUCATION®

V 3.2